The **LUMINAR NEO HANDBOOK**

The Ultimate Software Companion for Photographers

by Nicole S. Young

www.nicolesy.com

THE LUMINAR NEO HANDBOOK

THE ULTIMATE SOFTWARE COMPANION FOR PHOTOGRAPHERS

by Nicole S. Young

Published by Nicolesy® Inc. | www.nicolesy.com
Copyright © 2023 Nicole S. Young, All Rights Reserved

Copy editor: Linda Laflamme
Layout, Design, and Photography: Nicole S. Young

NOTICE OF RIGHTS

All rights reserved. No part of this book may be reproduced, stored in a retrieval system, or transmitted in any form or by any means without the prior written permission of the publisher, except in the case of brief quotations embodied in critical articles or reviews.

LIABILITY

The information in this book is distributed on an "As-Is" basis, without warranty. Neither the author, the publisher, nor the companies owned by the author shall have any liability to any person or entity with respect to any loss or damage caused by or alleged to be caused directly or indirectly by the instruction contained in this book or by the websites or products described in it.

TRADEMARKS

Many of the designations used by manufacturers and sellers to distinguish their products are claimed as trademarks. Where those designations appear in this book, and Nicolesy®, Inc. was aware of a trademark claim, the designations appear as requested by the owner of the trademark. All other product names and services identified throughout this book are used in editorial fashion only and for the benefit of such companies with no intention or infringement of the trademark. No such use, or the use of any trade name, is intended to convey endorsement or other affiliation with this book. Adobe® Photoshop® is a registered trademark of Adobe Systems Incorporated in the United States and/or other countries. THIS BOOK IS NOT AUTHORIZED, ENDORSED, OR SPONSORED BY ADOBE SYSTEMS INCORPORATED, PUBLISHER OF ADOBE® PHOTOSHOP®.

ISBN-13: 978-1-960570-59-8

ABOUT THE AUTHOR

Nicole S. Young is a professional photographer and published author whose love of photography and teaching has grown into an online business, creating training materials and resources for other photographers. Nicole is best known for her books on food photography but is widely versed in various photographic genres, including nature, landscape, travel, and lifestyle. Nicole lives in the beautiful state of Oregon, USA.

Learn more about Nicole on her website — nicolesy.com

GET THE PDF EBOOK

If you are interested in a **PDF eBook version of this book**, please visit nicolesy.com/shop to get the digital version in both vertical and horizontal formats. This version can be viewed on any device where PDFs can be read.

Save 20% with the code: LUMINARNEO

CONTENTS

INTRODUCTION	**2**
CHAPTER 1: CATALOG	**4**
The Catalog Module	4
The Catalog Workspace	6
CHAPTER 2: PRESETS	**20**
Presets Module Overview	20
The Presets Workspace	22
Apply Presets	24
Importing Presets	25
Creating Presets	27
CHAPTER 3: EDIT	**28**
The Edit Module	28
The Edit Workspace	30
Layers	33
Masking	37

CHAPTER 4: ADJUSTMENTS — 44

Adjustment Tool Panels — 44
Crop^{AI} — 45
Essentials Tools — 46
Creative Tools — 62
Portrait Tools — 78
Professional Tools — 84

CHAPTER 5: EXTENSIONS — 88

HDR Merge — 88
Focus Stacking — 90
Upscale^{AI} — 92
Noiseless^{AI} — 93
Supersharp^{AI} — 94
Magic Light^{AI} — 95
Background Removal^{AI} — 96
Panorama Stitching — 98

CHAPTER 6: FINAL TOUCHES — 106

Using Luminar as a Plugin — 106
Batch Processing — 112
Exporting from Luminar Neo — 113

CONCLUSION — 114
SHORTCUTS — 116
INDEX — 120

INTRODUCTION

WHAT IS LUMINAR NEO?

Developed by Skylum Software, Luminar Neo is an approachable and easy to use — yet extremely powerful — photography post-processing application. In it, you can organize your images within a catalog, process image files (including raw, JPEG, and more), add stylistic and AI-powered enhancements, mask, crop, work with layers, and so much more.

Some photographers choose to use Luminar Neo as their sole photography editing platform and create a catalog referencing all of their image files. Others use it as a plugin, where they do their main editing in one application — such as Adobe® Lightroom® Classic or Photoshop® — and then stylize the photograph by adding finishing touches inside of Luminar Neo. It's a fantastic program with a lot of options and is a great addition to any photographer's toolbox.

WHAT'S NEW IN LUMINAR NEO?

This product adds many new features and is a great addition to the Luminar family. Here are some of the standout additions to Luminar Neo:

- **Layers**: While using layers is not new to the lineup of Luminar products, the previous version (Luminar AI) does not have layers and is more focused on editing photographs. Luminar Neo now has all of the capabilities of Luminar AI but with powerful layering and masking added to it.
- **Portrait background removal**: Quickly remove the background from portrait images and replace it with a new background image.
- **Mask^{AI}**: Automatically select parts of your image, such as people, the sky, water, and more.
- **Objects removal**: Quickly remove unwanted objects, such as power lines and dust spots.
- **Extensions**: New to Luminar Neo are optional extension add-ons you can purchase and install to your application.

WHAT WILL I LEARN IN THIS BOOK?

This book is for photographers of all levels who are seeking a straightforward guide to help them incorporate Luminar Neo into their workflow. Throughout the pages of this book, you'll discover and learn about the following:

- Using the **Luminar Neo catalog** for viewing and organizing your image files.
- **Working with presets**, which includes creating your own and importing preset files you've downloaded to your computer.
- Utilizing the new **layers and masks features** in Luminar Neo's Edit module.
- Incorporating Luminar Neo **as a plugin** for Lightroom Classic, Photoshop, Apple Photos, and editing individual (non-cataloged) image files.
- **Batch-processing** your images to efficiently apply edits across multiple photos.
- Exploring and utilizing the brand-new **Luminar Neo extensions**.

By the time you finish this book, you'll be well-versed in using the majority of Luminar Neo's features and tools. Additionally, you'll have gathered some insights into how to leverage this software and incorporate it into your workflow to enhance your personal artistic creations.

VIDEO TRAINING

To further help you solidify your knowledge in Luminar Neo, I have provided a **start-to-finish video course** with downloadable image files so you can follow along and practice the steps. Here's how to access these files:

1. Visit this link: `https://nicolesy.com/neobook`
2. Use this special code to complete the form: `5f93-bas8-np72`
3. Check your email with instructions on how to access the course and download files.

CATALOG   1

The Luminar Neo catalog is where your files are displayed and organized so that you can locate, view, and sort the files you want to work with. If you use (or plan to use) Luminar Neo as your main photo editor, then you may want to consider creating a catalog so that your images are all visible in one place. However, it's not a requirement to use the catalog in order to take advantage of the software's presets and editing tools.

THE CATALOG MODULE

- **A** **Luminar menu**: Click to reveal a menu with common actions, such as updating and preferences.
- **B** **Search**: Click to open the search window.
- **C** **Module selector**: Navigate to the Catalog, Presets, or Edit modules.
- **D** **Sort and filter**: Sort and filter the photos in your catalog when in the grid view.
- **E** **Right sidebar toggle**: Click to toggle the right sidebar's visibility.
- **F** **Extensions installer**: Click to display a window where you can view and install the available Luminar Neo extension packs.
- **G** **Export**: Click to export the selected file(s).
- **H** **Add Photos**: Click to add photos to your Luminar Neo catalog.
- **I** **Shortcuts**: Displays shortcuts based on flags, date, and so on.
- **J** **Folders**: Shows all folders that have been added to the catalog.
- **K** **Albums**: A list of all created albums.
- **L** **Image preview**: Displays the image in either grid view or single image view.
- **M** **Info panel**: Displays image information, such as filename, camera, and exposure settings.
- **N** **Photo actions**: Click to flag an image (favorite), rotate, and copy/paste settings.
- **O** **Extensions**: View your installed extensions in this area, such HDR Merge, Focus Stacking, and Upscale.

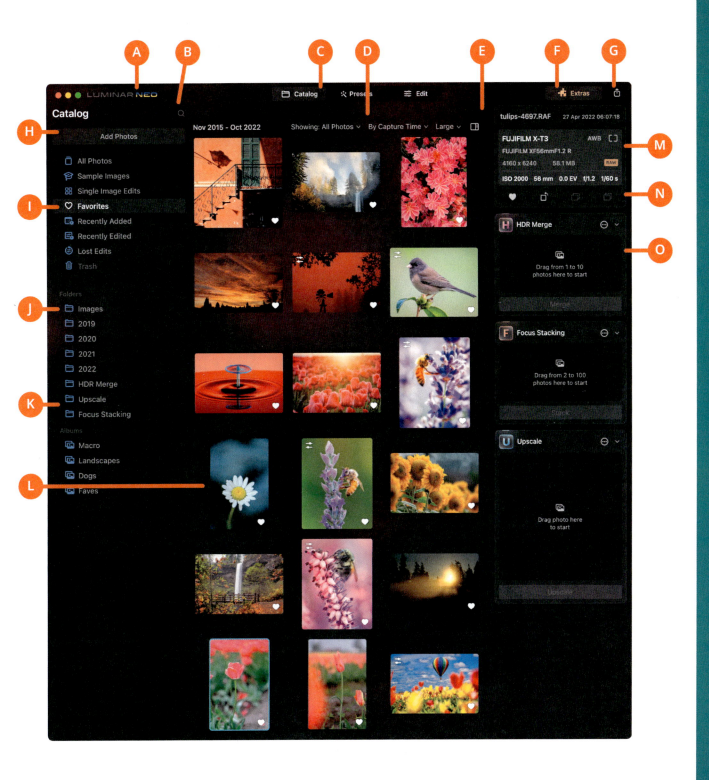

Chapter 1: Catalog

THE CATALOG WORKSPACE

Luminar Neo uses a catalog to keep your images organized when working in the standalone application. By default, photos initially added to this catalog are *not moved* or relocated from your hard drive. Instead, they are *referenced* in the catalog's database, and their original location is visible using the Folders drop-down. Your edits are saved to the catalog's database, which allows you to work non-destructively (meaning you are not editing the actual file, and the edits are saved alongside your original image).

You can have more than one catalog, which can be helpful if you wish to expand your organization beyond a single catalog with all of your photos. For example, if you work with clients, you may want to create a new catalog for each client. The method you choose to organize your catalog structure is up to you.

- **Create a new catalog**: To create a new catalog, in the menu, select ***File > Catalog > New***. Give your catalog a name, and set its location.

- **Open an existing catalog**: To open an existing catalog, go to ***File > Catalog > Open*** and navigate to the catalog on your computer.

- **Open recent**: If you have multiple catalogs, it might be difficult to locate them on your computer. Instead, you can quickly access recent catalogs using the Catalog menu. To do this, go to ***File > Catalog > Open Recent***.

HOW THE CATALOG SAVES EDITS

All editing and organizing you do in Luminar Neo will automatically save to the catalog, and when you are finished with your edit, the file can be exported which will embed all edits to a final image file (see *"Exporting from Luminar Neo" on page 113* to learn more). When you make changes to a photo, the data is stored in a hidden **.state** file type for each image to ensure that your entire catalog cannot be corrupted if data to one file becomes compromised.

LUMINAR PREFERENCES

If you ever discover Luminar Neo acting slower than expected, one place to check might be the Preferences (also referred to as Settings). This allows you to set your cache size, how often the catalog backs up, and more.

To open the Preferences, click the Luminar Neo menu drop down in the top-left corner of the application window and choose *Settings*.

- **Catalog Location**: This displays the location of your catalog and cache files. Click the folder to move the catalog's location.
- **Cache**: The *cache* stores preview images of your photos (the images you see in the preview window). If you have sufficient hard-drive space and you want to improve the speed of Luminar, you can set this to a higher number.
- **Auto Backup**: Set the maximum backup size, along with how often you want Luminar to back up the catalog.
- **Graphics**: The Graphics Processor helps to provide performance benefits when using photography-editing software such as Luminar Neo. Enable this setting to ensure that you have faster speeds and image rendering when editing and viewing your photos.
- **Analytics**: Decide if you want Skylum to collect anonymous data from your application to aid in analytics research.

Chapter 1: Catalog   7

BACKING UP & RESTORING THE CATALOG

With anything digital these days, it's important to keep backups of your work to ensure that you have a copy in case of hardware failure, damage, or catastrophic events. In Luminar Neo, your catalog will be regularly backed up to the same folder where the original catalog file is stored (learn how to adjust this setting on the previous page).

However, it's also a good idea to save a *manual backup catalog file* to another location from time to time to ensure you have an additionaly copy. This could be a physical hard-drive that is in a separate location from your main computeror a cloud-based online backup service. Either way, copy to it regularly. If something disastrous happens to your computer or hard drive, losing the catalog would mean losing all of your image edits and other changes to your photos. Creating a manual backup in Luminar Neo will help to ensure that your data remains safe.

BACKING UP THE CATALOG

Here's how you can manually create a backup of your Luminar Neo catalog:

1. In the menu, go to *File > Catalog > Backup*.
2. Choose the location where you would like to store the backup file and click **Save**.

    If you have a large catalog, this may take several minutes. Once it is complete you will have a separate backup copy of your Luminar catalog.

RESTORING A BACKUP

Here's how to restore a previously-saved backup of the catalog:

1. In the menu, go to *File > Catalog > Restore from Backup*.
2. Locate the backup file you created using the previous steps and click **Open**.
3. Luminar will prompt you to create and save a new catalog name. Give this catalog a new name and choose where you woud like to save it. (It's a good idea to give this catalog a different name than your previous catalog.)
4. When you are finished, click **Save** and your catalog will be restored.

ADD PHOTOS

The first thing you'll want to do with your new catalog is add photos. You can add photos that already exist on your computer or hard drive, or import (copy) new files from a memory card or external drive. Here's how:

ADD EXISTING IMAGES TO THE CATALOG

Adding photos to the catalog references the files in their original location and does not copy or move them to a new location. Here's how to add existing images and folders to your Luminar Neo catalog:

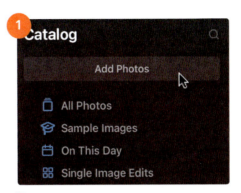

1. Click the *Add Photos* button on the top-left of the window.
2. Navigate to the folder of images, you wish to add, and click **Add**.

    The photos in the catalog will display in the same folder hierarchy they were originally assigned on your computer.

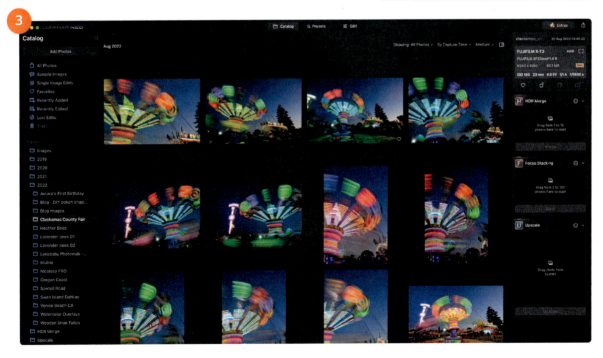

Chapter 1: Catalog   9

IMPORT NEW PHOTOS FROM A MEMORY CARD

Importing photos to a folder in the catalog copies the files to their new location. This method can be used for memory cards (SD, CF, etc.), as well as copying images from other locations and hard drives to create a new version of the files in the folder specified using the steps below. Here's how:

1. In the Folders section, click the **+** icon, and create a new folder where you want your photos to import into or locate an existing folder that already exists in the catalog. Alternately, you can add a subfolder to an existing folder by right-clicking that folder and choosing *New Subfolder*.

2. Connect your memory card to your computer.

3. Right-click the folder you want to import into, and choose *Import Images to this Folder*. The photos will be added to the computer folder you specified in Luminar.

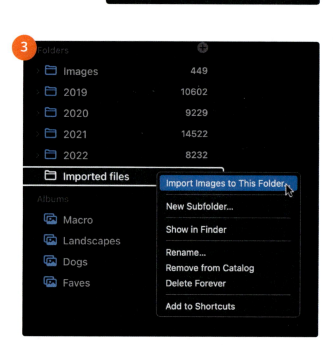

SEARCH THE CATALOG

You can use the search feature to locate photos in your catalog based on their filename, folder name, file extension (JPG, DNG, etc.), or date. To use the search feature, click the search icon in the top-left section of the window. Then, type out your request.

- **File and folder name**: Start typing the file or folder name, and the results will populate below the search box. Click the option you wish to view from the results below the search box.

- **Extension**: You can search for images based on their extension. For example, if you want to locate your raw files, you can type the file extension — such as *.raf*, *cr2*, etc. — and Luminar will display all files with that extension.

- **Date**: You can search the catalog based on the date something was created (this information is pulled from your file's metadata). You can either enter a specific date or be less specific. For example, if you want to find images created on a specific day but don't recall the year it was created, you can type the month and day (or simply the month), and it will give you results to choose from based on the year.

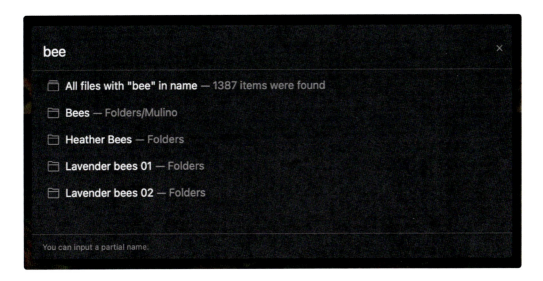

Chapter 1: Catalog   11

SHORTCUTS

At the top-left part of the window is an area to view shortcuts to access your images, organized and sorted based on certain specifications. Some options below may be hidden if you have no photos in the shortcut category. You can also add folders and albums as a shortcut for easy access.

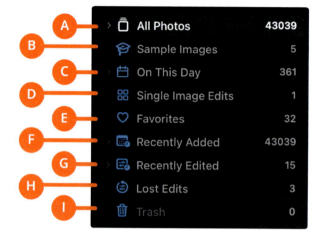

A **All Photos**: Displays all photos in your catalog. Clicking the small arrow to the left will reveal a timeline view of your photos based on the creation date of each image.

B **Sample Images**: Includes photos you can play with to test out Luminar Neo's features.

C **On This Day**: This displays all photos created on today's date from previous years.

D **Single Image Edits**: This shows all images that were edited without first adding them to the catalog. You can edit a single image using *File > Edit Single Image*. The file will appear in this shortcut but will not be added to the catalog.

E **Favorites**: This shows all photos that you have added as a favorite. To add a favorite, select an image, press **P** on your keyboard, or click the *heart icon* in the lower-left part of the image thumbnail.

F **Recently Added**: This shows a list of photos you recently added to the catalog. Clicking the small arrow to the left will display a list of dates you can click to show images imported on that date.

G **Recently Edited**: Displays all photos that had edits applied to them. Clicking the small arrow to the left will display your images based on when they were edited (*Today*, *This Week*, and *This Month*).

H **Lost Edits**: This shows any photos that have been edited in Luminar Neo but can no longer be found in their original folder. This can happen if an image was moved or deleted from the original location outside of the Luminar catalog. You will also see a small exclamation icon in the upper-left part of the image as a visual indicator of the image's "lost" status.

If the file still exists on your computer, you can locate these files to remove them from this shortcut. To do this, right-click the file and select *Locate Image*. Navigate to the image location, and the image edits will sync back to the original photos.

You can also delete the image edits in Luminar Neo by clicking the *Delete Lost Edits* button. This removes the edits from the missing photos so that they will no longer appear in this shortcut category.

I **Trash**: Adding photos to the trash will hide them from your catalog. If you want to permanently delete the files, click the Trash shortcut and then click the *Empty Trash* button at the top. This will delete the photos from both the Luminar Neo catalog, as well as your computer. Ensure you use this feature cautiously to avoid unintentionally deleting photos from your computer.

FOLDERS

All photos added to the catalog will display in their folder view on the left. This folder view mirrors the same folder structure where the photos exist on your computer or hard drive. You can use the + icon to add new folders, or right-click one of the folders to access the following options:

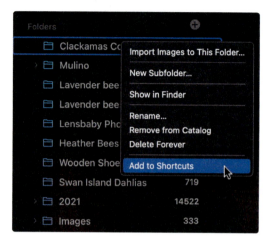

- **Add folder**: Creates a new folder on your computer.
- **Import Images to This Folder**: Allows you to copy files to the selected folder, either from a memory card or from other locations on your computer.
- **New Subfolder**: Creates a new subfolder on your computer.
- **Show in Finder (macOS) or Explorer (Windows)**: Reveals the original file location on your computer.
- **Rename**: Change the name of the folder.
- **Remove from Catalog**: Removes the folder from the catalog. This action does *not* delete the folder; instead, it removes it from the database, but the folder and files remain in their original location.
- **Delete Forever**: Deletes the folder from both the catalog and your computer.
- **Add to Shortcuts**: Adds the folder to the shortcuts section at the top.

ALBUMS

Albums are a way for you to organize your images at the catalog level. This means that images will not be moved on your computer but will be referenced in a new file structure in the catalog. Albums work well for organizing photos that are contained in different folders. For example, you might want to create an album that contains your favorite macro or landscape photos. Right-clicking an album gives you a few more options to work with:

- **Rename**: Change the name of the album.
- **Delete**: Deletes and removes the album from the catalog. This action does *not* delete photos or files.
- **Add to Shortcuts**: Adds the album to the shortcuts section at the top.

FILTER AND SORT

Just above the thumbnail view, you have options to sort and filter your photos:

A Choose to view all photos, only raw photos, only images you have flagged or rejected, or only the images you edited.

B Sort your images using several options, including capture time, file size, file name, file type, etc.

C Change the thumbnail sizes in the preview window.

Chapter 1: Catalog   15

INFO

Use the Info panel to view more information about your selected photo. This panel gives information such as filename, creation date, camera model, lens, white balance setting, exposure mode and settings, file size, and file type. You can also perform actions to your image, such as adding it as a favorite, rotating the image, and copying/pasting edits across images.

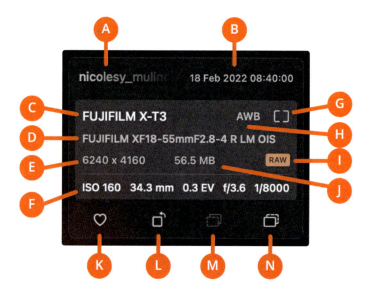

A   Image filename
B   Creation date
C   Camera model
D   Lens
E   Image dimensions
F   Exposure settings
G   Exposure mode
H   White balance setting
I   File type if raw
J   File size
K   Favorite
L   Rotate left
M   Copy adjustments
N   Paste adjustments

ADDITIONAL IMAGE OPTIONS

In the preview area, right-clicking an image gives you more options to work with. You can access these options both within the Gallery view or Single Image view.

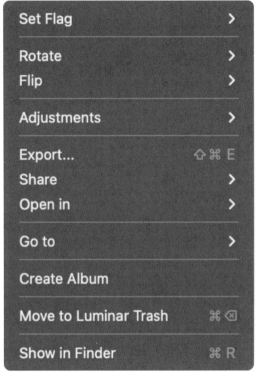

- **Set Flag**: Choose between Favorite, Rejected, or Unflagged.
- **Rotate**: Rotates the image left or right.
- **Flip**: Flips the image vertically or horizontally.
- **Adjustments**: Sync, copy, and paste adjustments, or reset all settings (***Revert to Original***).
- **Export**: Exports the image to your computer.
- **Share**: Shares the selected image (email, messages, etc.).
- **Open in**: Open the image in an external app.
- **Go to**: Go to other images created on the same date, or to the folder in the catalog.
- **Create (or Remove from) Album**: Create a new album with the selected image. Or, remove the selected image from the active album.
- **Move to Luminar Trash**: Move the photo to the trash in Luminar Neo, which does not immediately delete the photo. To permanently delete the image from your computer, access the Trash from the Shortcuts on the left and click ***Empty Trash***.
- **Show in Finder/Explorer**: View the original image on your computer.

VIEW AND SELECT IMAGES

The image preview area is where you will view and select the image(s) you want to work on. In this mode you have two ways to view your files: *Gallery* view and *Single Image* view:

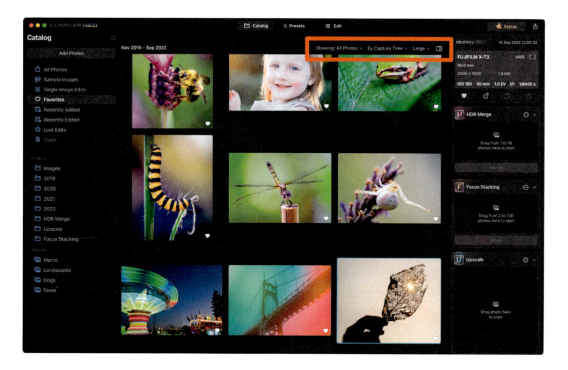

Gallery

In this view, your images will appear as a grid. This is a good way to scroll through images to select images you wish to organize, favorite, or edit. Here are some tips on working with images in the Gallery view:

- **Access Gallery view**: To access the Gallery view quickly from any module, press the `L` key.
- **Change thumbnail size**: Use the drop-down from the options above the image preview to set the thumbnail size: **Small**, **Medium**, **Large**, and **Largest**.
- **Select multiple images**: To select multiple images at once, press and hold the `COMMAND` (macOS) or `CTRL` (Windows) key and click the images you want to select.

SINGLE IMAGE

Viewing an image on its own can be useful to do things such as check focus and get a better idea of whether or not the image is something you want to take action on. You can quickly view an image in Single Image view by either double-clicking the thumbnail in the Gallery view, or by pressing the **SPACEBAR**. Here are some tips on using the Single Image view mode:

- **Photo Actions**: Below the image at the bottom of the preview are actions you can apply to your photo. If you don't see the Photo Actions, in the menu, go to *View > Show Photo Actions Panel*. (Note: This menu item is available only when in the Single Image view.) These actions show the full filename of your image, allow you to favorite or reject your image, toggle the before-and-after preview, as well as change the zoom level of the preview area.

- **Scroll through images**: Use the **RIGHT AND LEFT ARROW KEYS** to scroll through your images (these shortcuts also work in Gallery view).

- **Return to Gallery view**: If you want to jump back to Gallery view, you can either press the **SPACEBAR**, which will toggle your view between Gallery and Single Image. Or, use the keyboard shortcut **L** to go to the Gallery view.

PRESETS

2

Presets are a big part of Luminar Neo's workflow. You can begin with a preset to get a good starting point for your edits or add a preset to create a unique style or effect. In this chapter, you'll learn about the structure of the Presets module, along with how to import, apply, and create your own presets to save for future use.

PRESETS MODULE OVERVIEW

- **A** **Luminar menu**: Click to reveal a menu with common actions, such as updating and preferences.
- **B** **Module selector**: Navigate to the Catalog, Presets, or Edit modules.
- **C** **Extensions installer**: Click to display a window where you can view and install the available Luminar Neo extension packs.
- **D** **Export**: Click to export the selected file(s).
- **E** **For This Photo**: Luminar Neo scans your photo, searches your installed presets, and adds recommended preset packs in this section. Scroll to the right to see more.
- **F** **My Presets**: This is where the user-created presets are stored. This section is hidden if no presets have been created by the user.
- **G** **Purchased**: All presets you have purchased and/or imported from an *.lnpc* file will be located here.
- **H** **Presets categories**: Luminar Neo comes pre-installed with several presets you can use. Scroll down to view all presets categories available in this program.
- **I** **Before/After comparisons**: Click the eyeball **Preview** icon to toggle the before-and-after comparison of your image, or the **Before/After** button to see a side-by-side split view.
- **J** **Zoom**: Change the zoom level of your image.
- **K** **Actions**: Click to reveal the option to either **Revert to Original**, which removes all Luminar Neo edits, or **Save as Preset**, which takes your edits and turns them into a preset in the *My Presets* category.

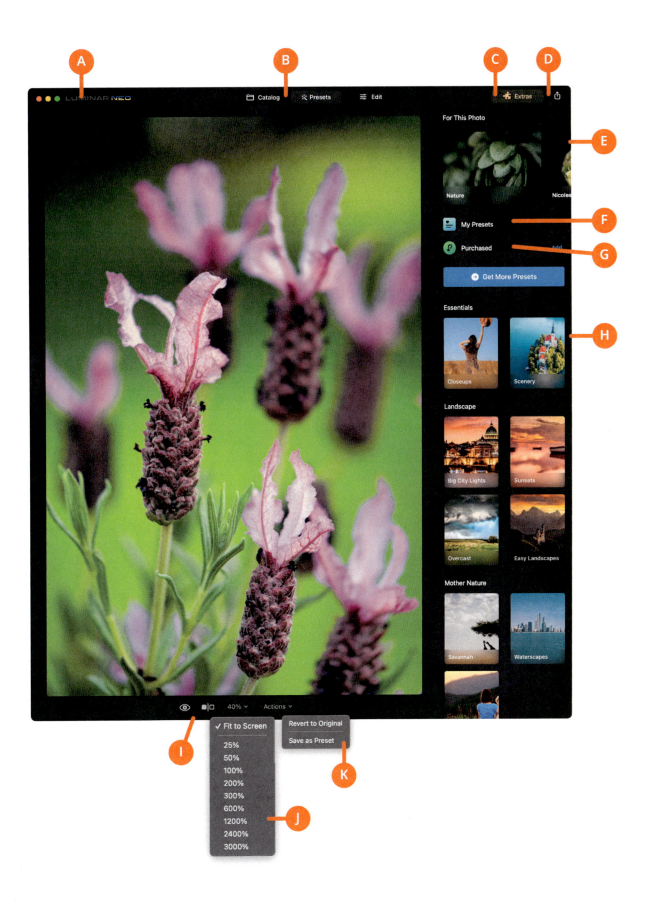

THE PRESETS WORKSPACE

PRESETS CATEGORIES

The categories for all presets are listed on the right side of the window when inside the Presets module. You'll notice at the top that there is a section titled *For This Photo*. This section uses AI to help determine a preset pack that might work well with your image and displays a handful of these packs from your collection.

If you scroll down towards the bottom of the window, you'll see groups of preset types, such as *Essentials*, *Landscape*, *Portrait*, and so on (**A**). Scroll all the way to the bottom to reveal a list of all categories (**B**). The presets in these lists are default presets that come pre-installed in your software.

MY PRESETS

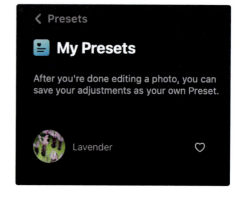

Near the top of this sidebar is a section titled *My Presets* (**C**). This section is visible when you have created your own presets from within the application, or if you have imported individual presets you downloaded from online.

PURCHASED PRESETS

The *Purchased Presets* section displays all presets that were downloaded and imported into the Luminar Neo program. These include presets you purchase directly from Skylum, along with other presets using the **.lnpc** file type.

Clicking the **Get More Presets** button will take you to the Skylum marketplace where you can purchase even more presets. Or, visit the Nicolesy Store (**nicolesy.com/store**) to see some from my own collection, including texture overlays, LUT files, and creative color and black-and-white effects.

APPLY PRESETS

To apply a preset to your photo, simply select the photo you want to work on, choose the preset category you want to use, and then click a preset from the list. Here are some tips and more information on working with presets in Luminar Neo to help you get the most out of the Presets module:

- **Hover to preview the preset effect**: One nice feature in this program is the ability to preview a preset's effect before applying it simply by hovering over the preset name. The effect will display in your preview window over your image, but the preset will not be applied until you click it in the list.

- **Preset Amount Slider**: After applying a preset, you'll notice a slider just below the preset name. Moving this slider to the left will decrease the overall intensity of the preset you just applied. This works by decreasing the amount or opacity of the tools used to create the preset. For example, if a preset uses a texture, and you decrease the preset amount to 80%, the opacity of the texture layer will be decreased to a setting of 80%. This makes it easy to alter the intensity of your preset by simply going to the Edit panel and altering the adjustments.

- **Presets overwrite all Luminar edits**: One thing that is essential to keep in mind is that applying a preset will overwrite all of the edits you already applied to your in the Edit module. But don't worry! If you accidentally apply a preset, you can use the keyboard shortcut **COMMAND + Z** (macOS) or **CTRL + Z** (Windows) to undo your last command.

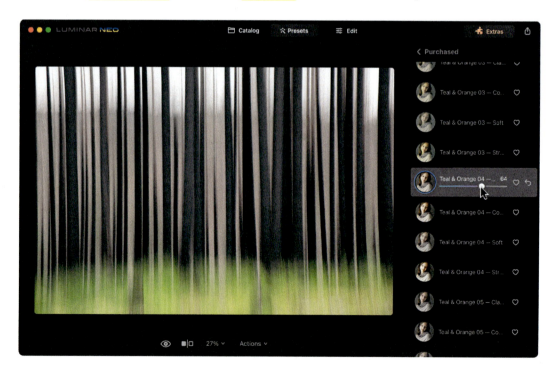

IMPORTING PRESETS

Imported presets will appear either in the *My Presets* or the *Purchased* section in the Presets module sidebar. The type of preset file you install will determine where the preset(s) will end up in this module.

LNP files:

An *.lnp* file is an individual preset that can be added to the *My Presets* folder. You can view all created and imported presets by accessing this section in the Presets module sidebar.

HOW TO ADD LNP FILES INTO LUMINAR NEO:

1. Click the *My Presets* section in the Presets module sidebar. If you don't see this section, first create a preset. Then, go back to the *Presets* module and continue with these steps.

2. Click the three dots next to one of the preset names and choose **Show in Finder/Explorer**. This will take you to a folder containing the information for that individual preset.

3. From this folder, go backwards once to the main preset folder. This folder will likely be called *Users* (or something similar). Copy and paste your **.lnp** files or folders into this folder, and your presets will appear in Luminar Neo.

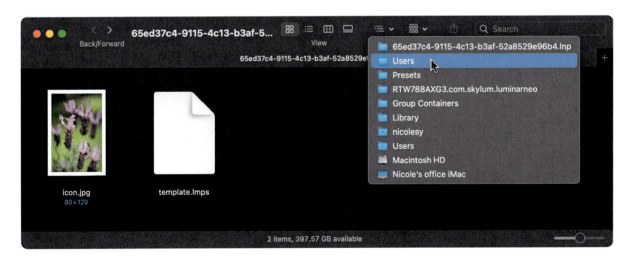

Chapter 2: Presets   25

LNPC files:

The *.lnpc* file is a collection of presets packaged together in a special file, making it easy to import a group of presets all at once. You will find these from presets downloaded using the Skylum marketplace or from some third-party sites who sell downloadable preset files for Luminar Neo.

HOW TO IMPORT THE LNPC FILE INTO THE PRESETS MODULE:

1. In the Luminar Neo menu, go to **File > Add Luminar Neo Preset Collection**.
2. Navigate to the **.lnpc** file on your computer and click **Open**.
3. Your new preset collection should now be installed in the Luminar Neo Preset module (**Purchased Presets** section). If you don't see it right away, you may need to quit and re-open the software and check again.

CREATING PRESETS

Creating your own presets is a great way to save a specific look to use on other photos. This can be helpful when working with a group of photos from the same photo-shoot and you want to make sure that the style is consistent, or to create a look to use later on other images. Here's how to get started creating your own presets in Luminar Neo:

HOW TO CREATE A PRESET:

1. The first step is to apply tools and/or layers (textures or overlays) to your photo using the **Edit** module.

2. Next, click the **Actions** drop down at the bottom of the window and select **Save as Preset**.

3. Your preset will be saved, and you will automatically be redirected to the Presets module. The preset will be saved with a small thumbnail icon of the image you used to create your preset. Now, rename your preset to give it a unique and easy-to-understand name.

CONSIDERATIONS WHEN CREATING PRESETS

When creating a preset in Luminar Neo, there are a few things to keep in mind. First, **all layers will be saved to your preset**. This includes tools, adjustments, layers, and masking to any added layers. Also, there are some tools and effects that will *not* save to a preset. This includes tools such as the Crop tool, Erase (Powerline and Dust spots removal), the advanced masking features (Mask^{AI}, Portrait Background, and Background Removal^{AI}), and the Extensions. These items will need to be applied manually to each photograph.

EDIT

3

The Edit module is where the magic happens! This is where you can add and blend layers, crop your photo, apply and alter stylistic adjustments and effects, create your own presets, and more. In this chapter, I'll review how the Layers and Masking panels work, along with the Layer Properties panel, where you can transform and blend layers. In the next chapter you'll learn all about the Tools and Edit panels. *Please turn to "Adjustments" on page 44 to learn more.*

THE EDIT MODULE

A **Layers**: Add, select, rearrange, and delete layers.

B **Module selector**: Navigate to the Catalog, Presets, or Edit modules.

C **Extensions installer**: Click to display a window where you can view and install the available Luminar Neo extension packs.

D **Export**: Click to export the selected file(s).

E **Tools tab**: A list of all tools available in the Edit module.

F **Edits tab**: The list of tools that have been applied to the photo.

G **Layer Properties^{PRO} & Masking**: Use this panel to make adjustments to your layer, including Opacity, blend modes, and masking.

H **Crop^{AI} tool**: Crop, rotate, and flip your photo.

I **Favorites**: Tools added by right-clicking and "favoriting" for easy access.

J **Extensions**: The Noiseless^{AI}, Supersharp^{AI}, and Magic Light^{AI} extensions.

K **Essentials tools**: Add essential and corrective effects, such as color adjustment, black-and-white conversion, vignettes, erasing dust spots, and more.

L **Creative tools**: Creatively style the color and tone in your photographs, and apply other effects (sun rays, fog, and more).

M **Portrait tools**: Tools for working with images of people.

N **Professional tools**: Advanced image tools to take your photos to the next level.

O **Before/After comparisons**: Click the eyeball **Preview** icon to toggle the before-and-after comparison of your image, or the **Before/After** button to see a side-by-side split view.

P **Zoom**: Change the zoom level of your image.

Q **Actions**: Click to reveal the option to either **Revert to Original**, which removes all Luminar Neo edits, or **Save as Preset**, which turns your edits into a preset in the *My Presets* category.

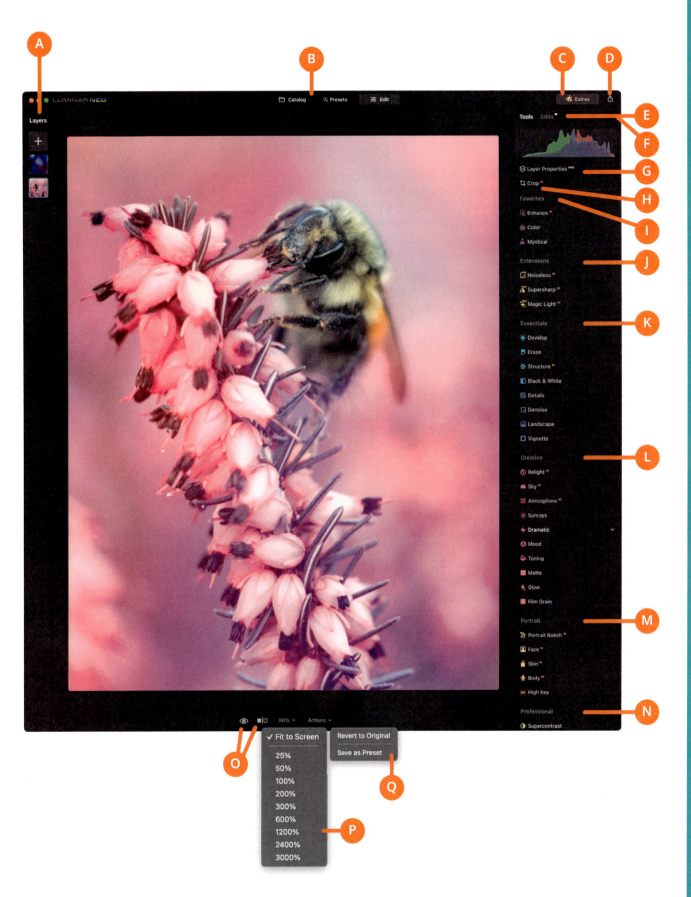

Chapter 3: Edit

THE EDIT WORKSPACE

The Edit workspace consists of three main sections: *Layers*, *Tools*, and *Edits*. In this chapter, I'll give you an overview layers and masking. Then, in the next chapter, we'll dive deeper into the tools and adjustments each offers and how they work with your images.

EDIT WORKSPACE SECTIONS

The Edit workspace consists of these three main sections:

- **Layers**: Working with layers in Luminar Neo allows you to add textures, apply watermarks, and create simple composite photographs. This section works together with the *Layer Properties* panel on the right side of the Edit module to allow you to change the Opacity and blend mode, apply masking, as well as flip the layer and "map" the layer to your image so it fits properly.
- **Tools**: The Tools section in Luminar Neo is where the magic happens. Here you can crop your photo, add tone and color adjustments, and work with the Luminar Neo extensions.
- **Edits**: This section displays all edits that you have applied to the active layer from the Tools section, with the most recent edit added to the top.

THE HISTOGRAM

The histogram is only visible within the Edit module while viewing the Tools section. To view the histogram, in the menu, go to *View > Show Histogram*. This will make it visible at the top, just above the Layer Properties.

WHAT IS THE HISTOGRAM?

A histogram is a graphical representation of the colors and tones in your photo. The far left side of the graph represents dark areas, the far right side of the graph represents bright areas, and the middle section represents the midtones. There is no correct histogram, nor is there a specific shape of graph that you should aim for. A histogram is merely a representation of the colors and tones in your image and works as a tool to help you understand your image edits more effectively.

By default, you will see a full histogram with all color spectrums (red, green, and blue), along with the tone graph layered with it. But you can easily view each histogram on its own simply by clicking the histogram in the application. This will cycle through all of the histogram states so you can view them on their own. Below are some examples of photos and their histograms to give you a better visual on how this works.

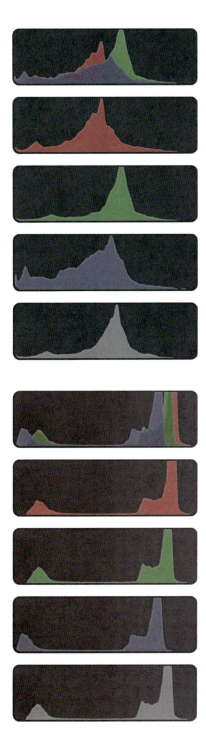

In the histogram of this frog image, most of the graphs are weighted in the center and to the left. This indicates that there is not a lot of overly bright or white parts of the photo, and the exposure is fairly even across the entire scene. The green in the graph is also weighted slightly heavier than the other colors, which make sense due to the amount of green colors in the photograph.

The photo above has a lot of contrast, which is represented well in the histogram. Notice that there is very little area of the graph for all colors and tones in the center of the histogram, and most of it is visible on the far left and right sides.

VIEWING HIGHLIGHTS AND LOWLIGHTS

When working with the editing tools, you will likely want to prevent "clipping" the highlights and lowlights. Clipped areas of a photo are spots that have pure white or black, sometimes resulting from overexposure in the camera or from over-processing. In the histogram graph, this is represented with the graph pushed up to the far left or right of the histogram. Anything that is pushed too far so it is flush up against the right or left sides means that it is clipped.

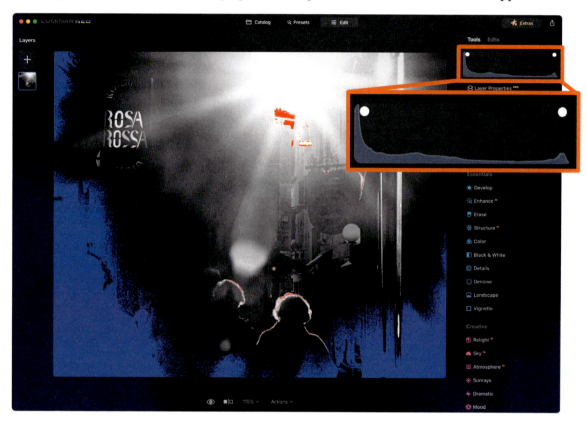

You can visualize these areas by toggling the clipping options, located in the histogram. In Luminar Neo, they are referred to as "Cold Pixels" for clipped lowlights, and "Hot Pixels" for clipped highlights. Here's how to do this:

1. Hover over the histogram with your cursor. You will see two hollow circles appear near the top right and left corners.

2. Click one (or both) of these circles to activate the clipping visuals:

    → Activating the *left* circle will toggle the lowlight clipping, and will show any area that is completely black in a *blue overlay*.

    → Activating the *right* circle will toggle the highlight clipping, and will show any area that is completely white in a *red overlay*.

LAYERS

When you want to have more control over your image, combine more than one photograph together, or add effects such as textures and overlays, then you will want to work with layers. Combining layers with masking — which is the ability to hide or reveal specific areas of a layer — gives you an even more powerful arsenal at your fingertips.

THE LAYERS SECTION

On the left side of the application is the Layers panel. This is where you can add textures, overlays, image files, and more. Each layer acts as its own separate entity where filters can be applied independent of other layers.

ADDING A NEW LAYER

Here's how to add a new layer in Luminar Neo:

1. In the *Layers* panel on the left, click the **+** icon (**A**).
2. Next, choose the image you want to add to your document (**B**):
    - Luminar Neo comes pre-installed with several overlays you can apply to your photos. You can choose one of these from the list below to see the effect. To see more options from each category, click the **See all** text to reveal all available overlay layers from that group.
    - To add your own image layer, click **Load Image**. Locate the file on your computer and click **Open**. The image will appear as a thumbnail in the My Images category.
3. Click the thumbnail to apply it as a new layer to your photo. The new layer will be added and active in the Layers section (**C**).

Chapter 3: Edit 33

LAYER ACTIONS

To make changes to the layers in your Layers panel, or to duplicate an existing layer, you'll want to make use of the layer actions. These can be accessed by right-clicking the layer you want to modify.

- **Hide/Show Layer**: If you would like to hide the layer (or show a previously hidden layer) then you can choose this option. This setting is useful when you want to see how a specific layer affects your image without doing a full before-and-after preview.
- **Duplicate Layer**: This setting allows you to duplicate any layer within the Layers panel.
- **Remove Layer**: This deletes the layer from the Layers section.

In addition to the above actions, you can also *rearrange the layers* by dragging a layer up or down. The order of the layers can affect the look of the photo, so you may want to experiment with this to see how it affects your photos. This is particularly noticeable when working with layers that have different blend modes, as the blending will change how the layers interact, depending on what is above and below the active layer.

Take a look at the example below. This image has four layers on it. The top layer is a border and a stylistic lens flare layer just below it (**A**). If the lens flare layer is moved to the top of the layers panel, that layer now affects the border layer, whereas before it was covered up (**B**).

34   The Luminar Neo Handbook | Nicole S. Young

LAYER PROPERTIES

In the Tools section on the right side of the Edit module is an area called **Layer Properties**. This is where you can make adjustments to the active layer's opacity, blend mode, transformations, and more. Before making changes to this section, first you will want to ensure that the layer you want to edit is active in the Layer's panel (you will know it is active if it is highlighted with a blue outline).

OPACITY

The **Opacity** setting allows you to change the opacity of the entire layer. This is helpful when you want to reduce the intensity of an image layer. A setting of 100% means that the entirety of the layer is visible in the document, and lowering this percentage will reduce the layer's visibility. Oftentimes this setting is defaulted to 50% when adding new layers, so you may need to adjust it immediately after adding new layers to your document.

BLEND MODE

The Blend Mode setting — located just below the Opacity slider — allows you to change how a layer blends with the layers below. One common use of blend modes is when applying textures and overlays. While some blend modes do specific things for certain types of layers, oftentimes the results can be surprising. Experimenting with these settings is the best way to find the best blend mode for your image.

- **A** **Darken/Multiply/Color Burn**: Darkens and removes whites while retaining blacks.
- **B** **Lighten/Screen**: Lightens and removes blacks while retaining whites.
- **C** **Overlay/Soft Light/Hard Light**: Makes dark areas darker and bright areas brighter while ignoring most grays.
- **D** **Difference/Subtract**: A complex blend mode that typically creates an inverted look.
- **E** **Hue/Color/Luminosity**: Blends only the hue, color, or luminosity (brightness and contrast) in the layer.

Chapter 3: Edit   35

TRANSFORMATIONS & MAPPING

Just below the Blend Mode drop down is the option to flip your layer horizontally or vertically. You can also manually transform the layer by clicking and dragging the toggles on the corner of the layer within the preview area. These options allow you to resize and flip the layer so that it fits better with your image. This differs from the Crop^{AI} tool because it affects only the active layer and not the entire image canvas.

At the bottom of the panel are Image Mapping buttons that allow you to quickly fit the canvas to the layer in whichever way you see fit. Below are examples on how each of these buttons work.

This shows the image with a square texture added as a new layer.

Using the **Fit** button fits the texture layer inside the canvas while maintaining the layer's original proportions.

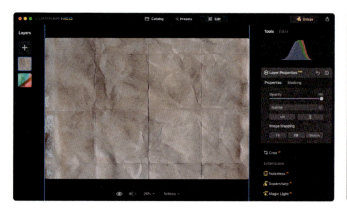

Using the **Fill** button fills the canvas with the texture layer while maintaining the layer's original proportions.

Using the **Stretch** button will fit the layer to the canvas and stretches the image so it takes up all space within the image.

MASKING

Masking is an important part of the photographer's workflow. With masking you can make selective adjustments, create composite images, and even replace a boring sky. Luminar's masking abilities, while straightforward, can be extremely powerful. Within this section I will discuss the tools and why you may want to apply them to your photographs.

WHAT IS MASKING?

Masking is ability to hide or reveal certain parts of a layer or adjustment without actually deleting any of the edits. It's a non-destructive and re-editable way to selectively adjust areas of a layer or adjustment, which is one reason it can be so powerful. If you're new to masking — and maybe even a little intimidated by it — this section will help to fill you in on all the basics to help you grasp what you need to know to use masking effectively in this software.

In Luminar Neo, the layer mask is represented by a red overlay while editing the mask. Wherever you see the red overlay, that part of the layer is visible — and the effect or layer is showing through — while all other parts of the mask are hidden. You can also mask your layer with a lower opacity, which is represented by a softer shade of red when viewing the mask. Doing this makes this area less visible, so the layer and its associated image edits will be more subdued.

This example shows a Radial Gradient mask added to an lens flare overlay layer. The red areas are where the layer will be visible, whereas all other areas will hide the layer.

Chapter 3: Edit   37

LAYER VS. ADJUSTMENT MASKING

There are two ways to mask in Luminar: You can mask the entire layer and also mask individual tool adjustments. *(Learn more about applying image adjustments on page 44.)* You'll notice that you have more masking options when working with layers versus adjustments. For example, when masking an adjustment, you will not see the **Portrait Background** or **Background Removal**^{AI} (if you have that extension installed). This is because some masks are only applicable at the layer level, whereas adjustment masking is more simplified.

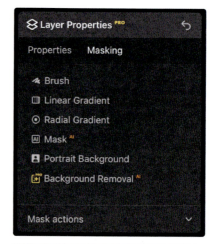

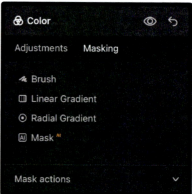

Layer Masking

Layer Masking — located within the Layer Properties panel — is ideal when you have more than one layer added to your image and want to selectively show or hide only certain parts of that layer. You can also use layer masking when combining more than one photograph to create a simple composite. Another use may be when adding textures and overlay layers to hide areas of the layer to make the texture or overlay less intense in that part of your photo.

The above panels show the difference between masking options when masking a layer (top) versus an adjustment (bottom).

In this example, I used layer masking to hide the light flare overlay effect that was covering up the horse.

Adjustment Masking

Most adjustments within the Tools panel can be masked on their own exactly as you would apply a mask in the Layers panel. This type of masking is ideal when you have one enhancement that you want to apply to only a portion of the image, such as masking a sharpening layer to affect only the eyes in a photograph while leaving all other adjustments as-is. The Masking section is visible on the top of each adjustment panel, with exceptions being the Crop^{AI}, Erase, Vignette, Portrait Bokeh^{AI}, Dodge & Burn, and Clone tools.

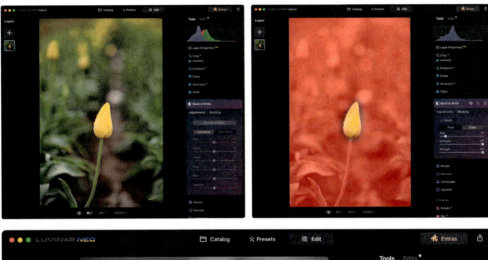

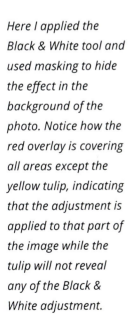

Here I applied the Black & White tool and used masking to hide the effect in the background of the photo. Notice how the red overlay is covering all areas except the yellow tulip, indicating that the adjustment is applied to that part of the image while the tulip will not reveal any of the Black & White adjustment.

TYPES OF MASKING

Luminar Neo has six different ways you can create masks in your image, including the optional Background Removal^{AI} extension (*turn to page 96 to learn how to use this feature*).

BRUSH

The **Brush** is the most basic tool for creating a mask. Using it is simple: You brush to either hide (Erase) or reveal (Paint) an area of a layer or filter. When active, the Brush tool has several options: **Size**, **Softness**, and **Strength**. These can be accessed either from the top part of the window or by right-clicking the image. *Softness* determines how soft or hard the edge of the brush will be, and *Strength* sets how opaque or translucent each brush stroke is as you sweep across. The image below shows examples of what the brush looks like at different settings.

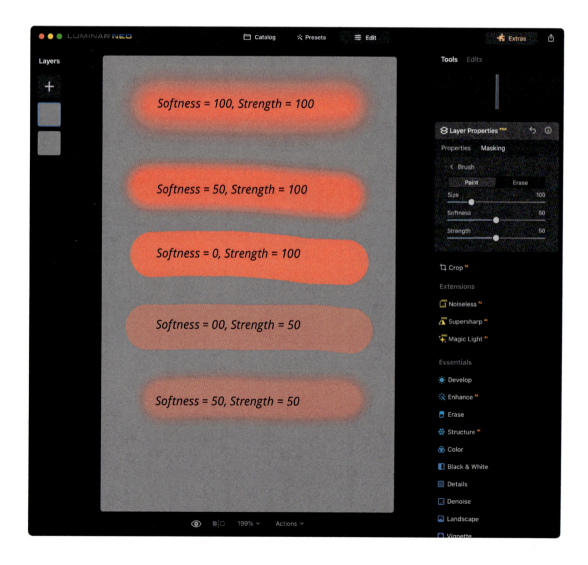

LINEAR GRADIENT

Linear Gradient masks work well when you want to add a feathered mask to the top, bottom, left, or right portion of the image. Some examples of using this mask are to darken a sky, lighten a foreground, or even blend together two images of the same scene photographed at different exposure settings. To use the Linear Gradient mask, select it from the list and start drawing your mask. This mask can be both inverted and resized after creating it for even more flexibility.

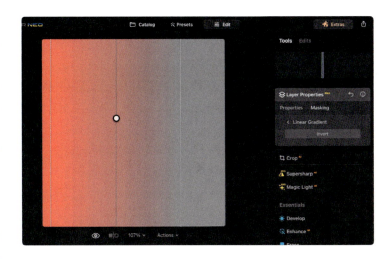

RADIAL GRADIENT

The *Radial Gradient* option adds a round, feathered gradient mask to an image. This is a useful tool when you want to create a quick and subtle perfectly round mask to one large area of an image to either hide or reveal an adjustment or layer. To create a Radial Gradient, select it from the list and start drawing a circle shape. This mask can be both inverted and resized after creating it for even more flexibility.

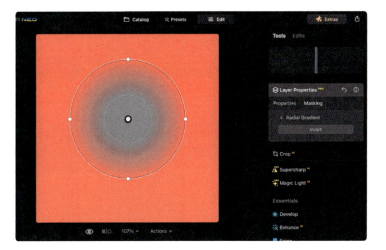

MASK^AI

When you want to create a more detailed mask but don't want to do the work yourself, *Mask*^AI is a great place to start. Luminar will analyze your image and give you options, such as Sky, Water, Mountains, and so on. Clicking these options will create a mask and apply the layer or adjustment to those areas. In this example, I selected the *Sky* and *Water* options from the Mask^AI list, which applied the Mood adjustment only to those areas.

PORTRAIT BACKGROUND

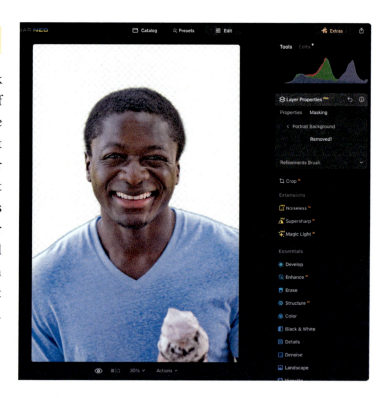

Portrait Background is a layer mask that removes the background of portrait images with one or multiple people clearly visible in the scene. It is accessible only through the Layer Properties panel. I find that I get the best results when the person is clearly in focus with minimal blur foreground or background blur, and good contrast between the person and background. It also works best with traditional-style portrait images.

To use the **Portrait Background** masking tool, first click it in the list Masking section of the Layer Properties panel. Luminar will analyze your image, and if a suitable portrait is found, you will see a Remove button. Click the button to remove the background. If the mask is not perfect (such as, if there are parts of the background still visible or parts of the portrait that were removed), you can manually adjust the mask using the Refinements Brush settings:

- **Transition**: This is the checkerboard area between the subject and its background. Brushing over the area between the object and background will further refine the transition area and give a better blend.
- **Object**: This area is represented by a light orange color. Toggle the setting in the panel and brush over the portrait (object) to make that area visible again.
- **Background**: This area is represented by a blue color. Toggle the setting in the panel and brush over the part(s) of the background that the AI did not remove to hide those areas from the mask.

MASK ACTIONS

After applying a mask to a layer or tool adjustment, you can use the additional controls to further enhance the mask. The best way to access these settings is to first create a mask, and then use the *Mask actions* section to view these options.

- **Fill**: This *fills the mask* and deletes any existing masking, revealing the contents on the layer or adjustment.
- **Clear**: Using this *removes the mask* and deletes any existing masking, hiding the contents of the layer or filter.
- **Invert**: This option *inverts the existing mask*.
- **Copy and Paste**: These are good options if you want to re-use a mask within a document. Luminar does not allow for copying and pasting masks between multiple open documents, however.
- **Show**: Clicking this button *toggles the visibility of the mask overlay*. The red color represents the visible areas of the mask, and anything that is see-through will hide that portion of the layer or adjustment.

ADJUSTMENTS 4

Adjustment tools are the heart and soul of Luminar Neo. They give you the ability to alter the color of your image, make the image darker or lighter, adjust raw settings, add a vignette, and so much more.

ADJUSTMENT TOOL PANELS

While each adjustment tool contains its own unique properties and slider settings, they all have some things in common. Before getting into the specifics of each tool and image adjustment, let's first review some of the shared features and settings in the adjustment panels:

- **Tool layout**: The tools in the list are organized into five categories: *Extensions*, *Essentials*, *Creative*, *Portrait*, and *Professional*. While most tools can be used on all images, some tools can be used only for specific image types (for example, the AI tools in the Portrait category).

- **Masking**: Many of the tools have the option to mask the adjustments applied with that tool. This allows you to apply an adjustment to only a specific area of your image. (*More information on masking tools can be found in the previous chapter on page 39.*)

- **The Edits section**: In the top-right sidebar you'll notice a section called Edits. This section displays all of the tools that have been applied to your image. If you want to make changes to a tool you already applied, this is where you will want to go to make those changes.

- **Multiple applications of tools and adjustments**: Many of the tools can be applied multiple times to the same photo. This allows you even more customization when working with the tools. You can intensify an effect by adding it more than once or to create a unique look with different variations of the same tool.

RESET ADJUSTMENTS

If you would like to **reset all settings** for an image and start over, the best way to do this is to access the Actions menu while in either the **Presets** or **Edit** view. Click the popup and select **Revert to Original** to bring your photo back to its original settings. You can also use the keyboard shortcut **COMMAND + SHIFT + R** (macOS) or **CTRL+ SHIFT + R** (Windows) with an image selected in the **Catalog** module.

To **reset an adjustment slider**, double-click the name of the slider to reset it.

CROP AI

The Crop AI tool allows you to crop, rotate, and flip your image. This tool affects the entire image (including all layers). *(If you would like to transform an individual layer, please turn to "Transformations & Mapping" on page 36.)* To crop your image, first activate this panel. You will then see a crop outline appear around your image. Then, use one of the handles along the edges of the photo to set your crop. You can also use the settings below for further refinement:

A **Ratio**: Set the ratio of your crop. By default, this setting will be set to Original, and the ratio will be locked. Changing the crop by moving the handles will maintain the original ratio of your photograph.

B **Transpose**: Change the orientation of the crop from horizontal to vertical (or vice versa).

C **Composition**[AI]: Clicking this button will automatically set the ratio and cropped area, based on the contents of your image.

D **Horizontal Alignment**: Click this button to automatically level the image's horizon.

E **Rotate & Flip**: Rotate the image, or flip your photo horizontally or vertically.

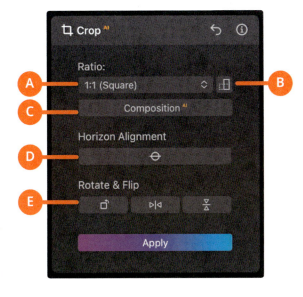

ESSENTIALS TOOLS

The **Essentials** adjustment tools will likely be your first stop for the majority of your photographic edits. Here you will be able to control the basic color, tones, sharpening, and other finishing touches.

DEVELOP

The **Develop** tool is going to be the starting point for most photographs, particularly with raw images, but it is just as useful with other image file types as well. This panel is where you can adjust the exposure, tone, and contrast for your images. By default you'll see some basic adjustments, but there are several other options below, including white balance, a curves adjustment, lens correction, and more.

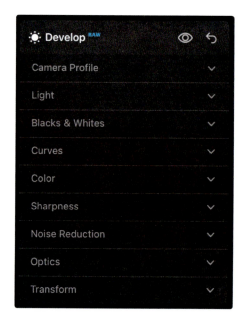

To reap the full benefits of a raw photograph's capabilities, you must use the Develop panel adjustments when you see the small blue **RAW** text alongside the adjustment's name. If this text is not visible in the main adjustment area and you are working with a raw file, don't worry! You can still access the original raw Develop tool in the **Edits** section. However, some of the sliders you see in this book will look different when you are not using the raw version of the Develop tool.

CAMERA PROFILE (RAW FILES ONLY)

Camera profiles help the software determine how to convert the colors in the raw photograph. It's best to use a profile that matches with your camera model. However, the *Luminar Default* setting works well when a matching profile is unavailable. *(If you would like to import a selection of camera profiles that Luminar Neo can use in the Develop setting, please turn to "Importing Custom Camera Profiles" on page 51.)*

LIGHT

The *Light* section helps you make adjustments and corrections to the brightness and contrast of a photograph. Here is an overview of what each slider in this section does:

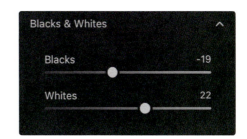

- **Exposure**: Make the image brighter or darker; allows you to correct for an under-exposed or over-exposed photograph.
- **Smart Contrast**: Increase or decrease the contrast.
- **Highlights**: Increase or decrease the intensity of the brightest areas of a photograph.
- **Shadows**: Increase or decrease the intensity of the darkest areas of a photograph.

BLACKS & WHITES

The *Blacks & Whites* section is a straightforward set of sliders that helps to increase or decrease the overall brightness and contrast in an image by focusing on two groups of tones: Whites and Blacks.

- **Whites**: Makes *bright areas* brighter or darker.
- **Blacks**: Makes *dark areas* brighter or darker.

CURVES

If you are unfamiliar with the *Curves* tool, at first it might seem intimidating. However, you'll find that it is a powerful and flexible visual tool that can help you achieve the balance and style you are looking for when it comes to both tone and color adjustments.

Simply move some points on a diagonal line to create a curve that shapes the shadows, midtones, and highlights just how you want. Plus, you can even fiddle with individual color channels to make your pictures pop with the perfect colors. Let's take a look at a few examples of how this works on the next page.

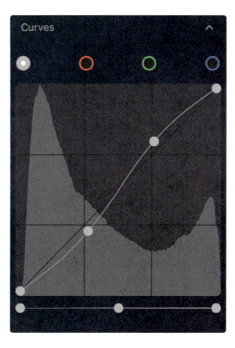

Chapter 4: Adjustments

When the curve is a **flat diagonal line** from the bottom-left to the top-right, it is inactive and does not have any style applied to it (**A**). Here are some key points to understand about how curves work:

- The area on the **right side** of the curve box represents the *bright areas* of the image.
- The area on the **left side** of the curve box represents the *dark areas* of the image.
- Moving a point **up** will make that area *brighter*.
- Moving a point **down** will make the area *darker*.

Adding a point and raising the line upwards will add brightness, and lowering the line will make an image darker. You can also add multiple points to create contrast effects. This effect (**B**) is called an S Curve. The top-right point is raised up, making the bright areas brighter, and the bottom-left point is lowered, making the dark areas darker. The more pronounced the "S" shape is, the more intense the contrast in the photo will be.

Creative tone effects can also be achieved quickly using curves. For example, moving the lower-left line directly upwards along the left edge of the curve will soften the blacks by making them brighter. Pair this with an S Curve for a trendy effect (**C**).

The color toggles can also be used to alter color in the image. You can intensify the Red/Cyan, Green/Magenta, and Blue/Yellow colors by adding points and moving them up or down on the curve line. In this example, I created an S Curve in the Red channel for an exaggerated split-tone effect.

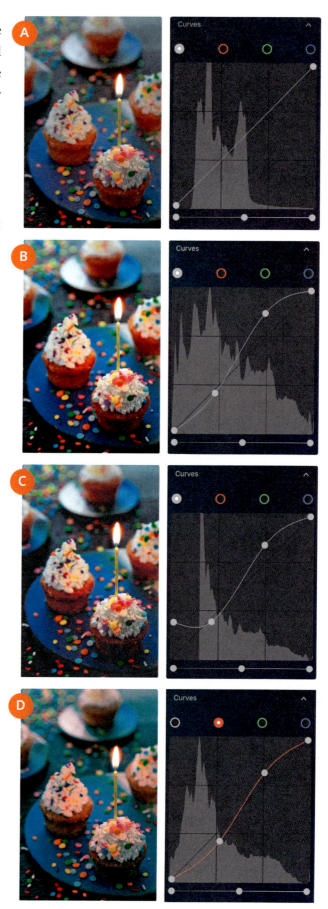

48   The Luminar Neo Handbook | Nicole S. Young

COLOR

This section allows you to adjust and correct the white balance in your photo. When working with a raw file, you have full control over this setting and are able to fine-tune the color exactly as you would like. However, you also can make alter the color with these sliders for other image types.

- **White Balance**: Presets to help you set the white balance according to the conditions of your photograph.
- **Eyedropper**: Click the eyedropper and click on a neutral color in your image (gray, for example) to set the white balance automatically.
- **Temperature & Tint**: Adjust the blue, yellow, green, and magenta colors.
- **Saturation & Vibrance**: Intensify the colors of your photo. Vibrance is less intense and will be gentler on the reds and pinks (including skin tones).

SHARPNESS

This section allows you to add simple sharpening to a photograph. It's aways best to zoom in to your image to see how the effect is being applied to prevent over-sharpening.

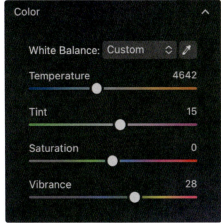

- **Sharpen**: This sets the overall amount of sharpening that is applied to your photo.
- **Radius**: Determines how much sharpening is applied to the edge of an area. The higher this is set, the more contrasty the edges within your image will appear, giving the perception of sharpness.
- **Masking**: By default, Luminar sharpens the entire image. The *Masking* slider allows you to restrict the masking to only the contrasty edges in a photo. The higher this slider is set, the more your sharpening will be restricted to these areas. This eliminates sharpening from areas with large groups of colors, such as blue skies or skin.

NOISE REDUCTION

Use the *Noise Reduction* section when your image is noisy or grainy and you want to smooth it out. Photos that were created with a high ISO setting or photographed at night tend to have more noise than those created with sufficient light for the scene. Be careful to not be too heavy handed with this setting or you'll lose realistic detail in your image. A little bit of noise in a photo is not a bad thing!

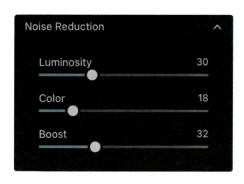

- **Luminosity**: Removes standard grayscale noise.
- **Color**: Removes color noise.
- **Boost**: Sets the aggressiveness of the noise reduction (similar to an "intensity" slider).

OPTICS

This section will help you remove distortions caused by certain lenses. When editing a raw photo, you will see all options available here. However, if you are editing a rasterized file (such as a JPEG, PSD, or PNG file), you will have limited sliders and other options.

- **Auto Distortion Corrections**: Removes distortion in a photo, typically resulting from a wide-angle lens.
- **Auto Fix Chromatic Aberrations/Auto Defringe**: Helps to remove any color fringing along the edges of objects in your image. This can be a result of poor-quality lens optics or shiny and contrasty items in the scene.
- **Lens Distortion**: Manually correct lens distortion in your photo. Moving the sider to the right will "stretch" the edges, whereas moving it to the left will pull the center of the image closer towards the frame. Careful, it's easy to add even *more* distortion when using this slider!
- **Devignette**: Some lenses add a subtle vignette along the edges of a photo. Use this slider to lighten the edges and remove the vignette.
- **Devignette Midpoint**: Moving the slider to the left will make the Devignette adjustment larger, and moving it to the right will push the Devignette setting closer to the edges of the frame.

TRANSFORM

Use this setting when your photo needs transformations that cannot be corrected using the Crop^{AI} tool. For automatic correction, click the button at the top of the section. You can also make manual adjustments using the sliders:

- **Vertical**: Corrects for vertical (up and down) distortion, such as a tall building or towering object photographed from below.

- **Horizontal**: Corrects for horizontal (left to right) distortion — for example, a flat object that was photographed at a slight angle when the image should be perpendicular.

- **Aspect**: "Squishes" the frame vertically or horizontally, depending on the direction you move the slider. This may be a necessary adjustment after applying a vertical or horizontal correction to help balance out the added distortion from manual adjustments.

IMPORTING CUSTOM CAMERA PROFILES

Here's how you can add a large collection of camera profiles to your computer so that Luminar Neo can access them in the Develop tool:

1. On your computer, type this link in your browser (**nicolesy.com/dng**) to download the Adobe DNG converter installation file.

2. Locate the downloaded file and open it by double-clicking the file.

3. Then, follow the prompts to install the DNG converter on your computer. (After it is installed, there is no need to open or use the DNG converter application.) The camera profiles will automatically be added to Luminar Neo under the Camera Profile section in the Develop tool.

One important thing to note is that not all camera models and file types are compatible with this download and will need to use the default Luminar and Adobe camera profiles (FUJIFILM .raf files, for example).

Chapter 4: Adjustments

ENHANCE^{AI}

One thing you'll find extremely useful in Luminar are the AI adjustment tools. With only a single slider you can make a huge visual impact on an image, and the *Enhance*^{AI} tool is a combination of several adjustments in one. With the **Accent**^{AI} slider you'll likely notice a change to the tone and contrast of your photo, but there are also some subtle color enhancements as well.

And, if you have a photograph with a sky in it, using the **Sky Enhancer**^{AI} will help boost the color and tones in the sky. The software is able to recognize skies (mostly blue skies) and performs corrections such as color, saturation, and even structural enhancements to clouds. It also masks around any foreground objects to prevent the adjustments from affecting parts of the image that are not the sky. But be cautious of being too heavy-handed with this slider, as it can add a halo effect along the edges of the horizon.

Before

After Enhance^{AI}

52   The Luminar Neo Handbook | Nicole S. Young

ERASE

The **Erase** tool helps you remove unwanted objects from your image. There are a few different ways you can use this tool:

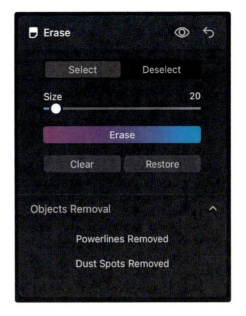

MANUAL SELECTION (BRUSHING)

With this method, you brush over the object or area you want erased. Set the **Size** slider to adjust the size of the brush. It's best to create a brush outline that is just a little bit larger than the object you want to erase. You'll see a red overlay on the area that you have selected. Then, when you're ready, click Erase and the objects will be removed.

You can also refine and reset this tool as needed. At the top, you'll see a toggle with **Select** and **Deselect** settings. By default it is set to *Select*, but you can remove brush strokes by toggling it to the *Deselect* setting. The **Clear** button will clear out any red brush strokes you have made so you can start over. Lastly, if you discover that there is an area you erased and you want to bring it back into view, simply brush over that area and click the **Restore** tool to bring back the original image.

OBJECTS REMOVAL

Luminar can automatically recognize and remove both *powerlines* and *dust spots* from a photo. Simply click the button for the appropriate object, and it will work its magic and clean up your photo.

Before

After Erase (Objects Removal)

Chapter 4: Adjustments

STRUCTURE ^{AI}

Another useful AI tool is **Structure** ^{AI}. This tool has two sliders. The **Amount** slider determines the overall strength of the structure effect. Moving it to the right will intensify the details in your image, whereas moving it to the left will apply a softening — and almost blurry — effect. The **Boost** slider will accentuate the details in your photo, giving the image an almost HDR look. One nice thing about this filter is that it is "human-aware" and tends to not over-process the skin and faces of people, giving them a much more natural look.

Before

After Structure ^{AI}

Before

After Structure ^{AI}

COLOR

The *Color* adjustment allows you to manipulate the hue, saturation, vibrance, and luminance of colors in your image. You can adjust many of these settings either globally (across the entire image) or to specific color groups using the **HSL** section. There is also a **Remove Color Cast** slider that is very helpful when you can see that the color is "off" but can't quite fix it with the white balance settings within the Develop panel. In fact, that small slider is probably one of my favorites in the entire application! It helps to clear away a "wash" of color in the image, such as a muddy brown or overly cool effect.

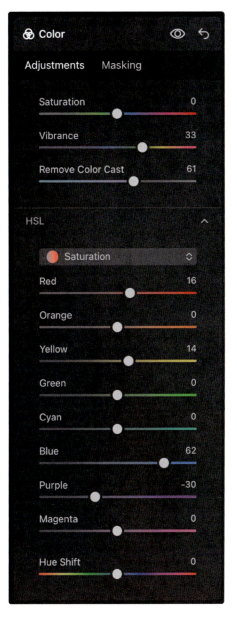

Before

After Color

Chapter 4: Adjustments

BLACK & WHITE

If you would like to convert your image to black and white, the *Black & White* adjustment is the tool to use. Simply click the **Convert to B&W** button, and the image will turn to grayscale. Then, use the **Luminance** sliders to either brighten or darken areas in the image based on their colors.

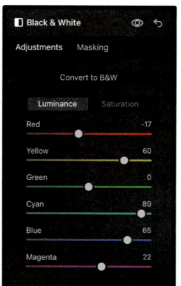 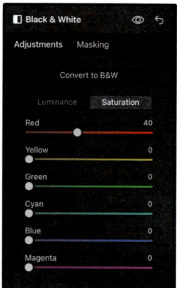

You can also bring color back into the image by using the **Saturation** sliders. This reveals color from your image, depending on the slider you are using. The sliders will go all the way to **100**, but if you want your original color to be revealed, only move the color sliders to a setting of **50**.

Before   *After Black & White (with Saturation adjustments)*

DETAILS

The ***Details*** adjustment will help you sharpen your photographs. There are a few things to keep in mind when sharpening a photograph. First, you can't sharpen something that is out of focus. If your image is blurry and has no point of focus, then no amount of sharpening will improve it. And second, this is one of those adjustments that you don't want to be too heavy-handed with. An over-sharpened photo is easy to spot and can start to look "crunchy" or grainy. Using a light touch is always the best approach when applying sharpening.

At a very basic level, sharpening is the process of adding contrast to the edges of elements within a photograph. Within Luminar there are several sharpening tools, and I'll go through a few of them here to help you understand what they can do with your photographs. This panel has a lot of sliders and can be a little bit confusing when you first start using it, but once you play with the sliders and really pay attention to your photograph, things will begin to become much more clear.

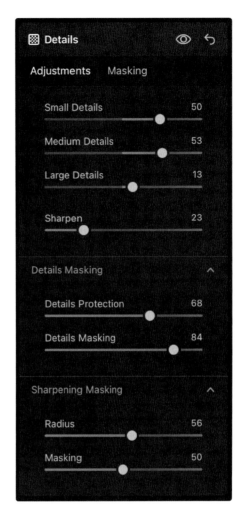

First, the most important thing you can do while sharpening your photographs is to zoom in to at least 100%. I tend to zoom in even further, typically to 200%. You also want to make sure that you are panning around the photograph and looking at all areas—both in-focus and out-of-focus—to make sure that you are sharpening only the parts of the image that you want to be sharpened.

Please note: In the example image on the next page, I've pushed many of the sliders well beyond what I would normally do while processing my own photographs. This is for demonstration purposes, (sharpening differences are sometimes difficult to see in small images in books) and also so that you can clearly see each effect in action.

- **Small, Medium, & Large Details**: These settings allow you to selectively control the small, medium, and large areas within your photograph.
- **Sharpen**: This is the standard sharpening slider, which will help to de-focus the edges of all items in your image.
- **Details Protection**: When using the Details sliders, increasing this slider can help your photo to not look over-processed.
- **Details Masking**: This slider will mask out areas of the image so that you have more control over what is affected.
- **Radius**: This setting will either increase or decrease the size of the sharpened edges. I like to think of this as an "intensity" adjustment.
- **Masking**: Adding masking to your sharpened image will help prevent large areas of solid color or out-of-focus regions from displaying any sharpened effects.

This shows the Details tool applied with each of the main sliders set to a high number to show how each slider affects the pixels in a photograph.

DENOISE

When you have a photo with a lot of noise or grain in it, the *Denoise* tool is very useful. The adjustment has three sliders: **Luminosity** removes grayscale (standard) noise, **Color** removes color noise, and **Boost** sets the aggressiveness of the noise reduction (think of it as an intensity slider).

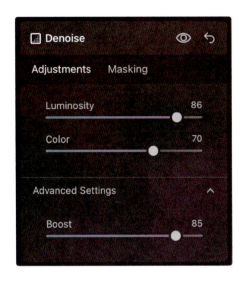

In the example below (zoomed in 200%), the image was photographed at ISO 12800, which introduced a lot of noise to the scene. By increasing the Denoise sliders I was able to remove most of the noise. However, moving them too far to the right can add a smudgy look, which is something you want to avoid. In fact, the example shows an excessive amount of noise reduction (far more than I would typically apply to my photos), but for demonstration purposes an appropriate setting would be so subtle it may not be visible in this book.

Before

After Denoise

Chapter 4: Adjustments   59

LANDSCAPE

The *Landscape* tool works well on any outdoor image with green foliage. This adjustment has four sliders: **Dehaze** helps to cut through haze by adding contrast, **Golden Hour** adds a touch of warmth, softness, and glow to the scene, **Foliage Enhancer** boosts the colors of foliage and greenery, and **Foliage Hue** lets you adjust the color (moving the slider left makes green foliage warmer, and to the right makes it more green).

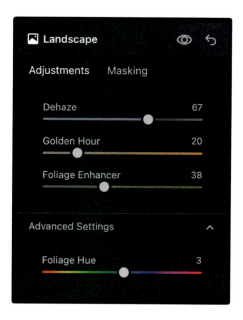

Before

After Landscape

VIGNETTE

A *Vignette* is a nice finishing touch to nearly all photos. Vignettes don't have to be intense; in fact, most of the time you probably won't even notice that a vignette was added to an image. However, they do help to subtly draw the eyes towards the main subject by darkening the edges of the image.

You can choose the type of vignette you want with the **Amount** slider (slide *left* for a dark vignette and *right* for a light vignette), and you can also adjust the **Size**, **Roundness**, and **Feather** (softness), as well as add **Inner Light** to the center of the vignette. To change the position of the its center, click the **Choose Subject** button and click on your image (good for off-center subjects).

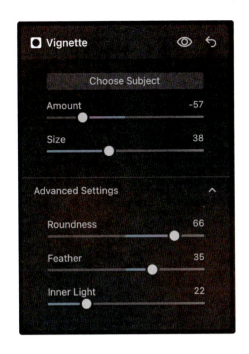

Before

After Vignette

Chapter 4: Adjustments

CREATIVE TOOLS

The *Creative* group of adjustments allows you to have some fun with your photos! Add a texture overlay, drop in a new sky, colorize with a LUT file, give your scene some gorgeous sunrays, and more!

RELIGHT^{AI}

The Relight^{AI} tool helps to correct for uneven lighting in the foreground and background of a photo. The tool will analyze your image and determine what the subject is. Then you can use the following sliders to adjust the light in your photo:

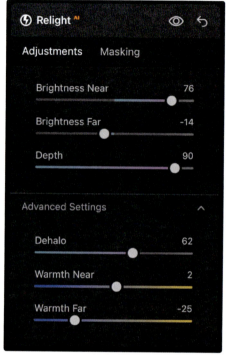

- **Brightness Near**: Increase the brightness in the subject or foreground of a photo.
- **Brightness Far**: Increase or decrease the brightness of the background.
- **Depth**: Move the spot where the background brightness starts from.
- **Dehalo**: Sometimes adding contrast to the subject and its background can give the subject a halo of light (or darkness) around its edge. Use this slider to minimize this effect.
- **Warmth Near/Far**: Increase or decrease the warmth of the subject (near) or background (far).

Before *After Relight^{AI}*

SKY^{AI}

The **Sky**^{AI} tool is an impressive adjustment that lets you drop in a brand-new sky to your image, and then masks all of the foreground elements automatically! Although the default placement works well, additional settings allow you to fully customize the position and look of your sky replacement.

To use this tool, first choose a sky from the **Sky Selection** drop-down list. There are several built-in options to use, and you can also add your own photo by selecting the **All Skies > Show Custom Skies** option; then, copy and paste your own sky images to the folder that pops up on your computer.

When choosing a sky to use, it's best to stick with the existing light and time of day of your photograph. For example, you wouldn't want to place a sunset sky in an image that was photographed mid-day. You will also want to take note of the sun position as well. If the light was behind you and your subject was lit from the front when you photographed it, for example, you should avoid a sky image where the sun is visible behind the clouds.

SKY ORIENTATION

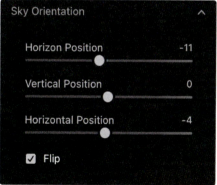

This section helps you position the sky to properly fit your scene. The AI functionality typically does a good job, but you may want to make some adjustments depending on your preferences.

- **Horizon Position**: This will move the position of the horizon (where the sky is blended) either up (move the slider to the right) or down (move the slider to the left). When adding a new sky, zoom in close to the horizon and analyze the blend to see if this setting needs to be adjusted.
- **Vertical Position**: Repositions the sky up or down (vertically).
- **Horizontal Position**: Repositions the sky left or right (horizontally).
- **Flip**: Flips the sky horizontally to improve the overall composition of your photograph.

MASK REFINEMENT

The AI does a good job of masking the subject and horizon, but sometimes minor adjustments are required to get a good result.

- **Global**: Think of this setting like a "feather" setting. Moving the slider to the right will increase the spread of the sky blend so that more of the sky will be overlapping the edge of the horizon. At a setting of 0 it still has a soft edge to it, but increasing the slider will make that edge even softer and add more of the new sky to the scene.

- **Close Gaps**: Sometimes you will see gaps and holes in areas of a photo, such as between trees or branches. Use this slider to help fill in and close those gaps to reveal more of the sky overlay in your background.

- **Fix Details**: This slider will help clean up small areas along the edges of objects where the original sky is still peeking through.

Before

Default Sky^{AI} Mask Refinement settings

Adjusted Sky^{AI} Mask Refinement settings

64   The Luminar Neo Handbook | Nicole S. Young

SCENE RELIGHTING

When you add a sky to an image, that new sky may have some tone and color differences compared to the rest of the image. The Sky^AI tool will light the scene to help blend the original image with the new sky.

- **Relight Strength**: Increase or decrease the intensity of the relight adjustment.
- **Relight Saturation**: Increase the amount of color from the new sky to the scene to help them look more cohesive.
- **Relight Human**: When people are included in the photo, this slider helps add realistic color balance to them so that they absorb some of the color of the new sky, creating a better overall blend.

Before

After Sky^AI Scene Relighting

REFLECTION

If you have a scene with water in it — such as a lake or river — you may need to use the Reflection settings to properly add water reflection to the scene.

- **Reflection Amount**: This will intensify the amount of sky that is reflected in the water. Move this slider to the right to make the sky more visible in the water's surface.
- **Water Blur**: This helps blend the reflected sky with water that is uneven or has ripples.

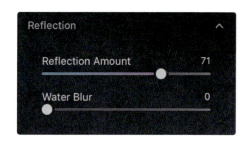

The Sky^{AI} tool with Reflection Amount set to 0

The Sky^{AI} tool with Reflection Amount set to 71

SKY ADJUSTMENTS

When adding your sky, you may need to make selective edits to the new sky so that it looks realistic with your photo. These sliders allow you to alter the look of the new sky in order to blend it better with your scene.

- **Defocus**: When working with a photograph that has a blurry background, you'll want to make sure that you also blur the new sky so that it looks natural. Increase this slider to achieve this look.

- **Grain**: Nearly all photographs have a slight amount of grain (or noise) in them. When adding a new sky, you may need to use this slider to match the original grain amount in your photo. This is also an essential slider to use after using the **Defocus** slider, because adding blur to a photo will remove any existing grain that was in the new sky image.

- **Atmospheric Haze**: This setting adds haze to the sky, which helps blend a new sky more naturally with your photograph.

- **Warmth**: Use this slider when the sky is too cool or warm for your scene. Move the slider to the left to make it cooler (blue), and to the right to make it warmer (yellow/orange).

- **Brightness**: Lastly, you can adjust the brightness of the sky to better match your overall image. Move the slider to the right to make the sky brighter, and left to make it darker.

Before

After Sky^{AI} Sky Adjustments (Defocus, Grain, and Warmth)

Chapter 4: Adjustments

ATMOSPHERE^{AI}

You can easily add fog, mist, or haze to a photo using the *Atmosphere*^{AI} tool. I find this tool works best with images that already have — or the conditions are appropriate for — fog, mist, or haze. Using this tool will help amplify and intensify the existing effect.

- **Mode**: Choose the type of atmosphere you would like to apply: *Fog*, *Layered Fog*, *Mist*, or *Haze*.
- **Amount**: Sets the intensity of the effect. Move the slider to the right to increase the amount of atmosphere in your scene.
- **Depth**: This will move the effect closer to the front of the frame (move the slider to the right) or further away and towards the back (move the slider to the left).
- **Lightness**: Move the slider to the left to make the atmosphere effect darker, or to the right to make it brighter.

Before

After Atmosphere^{AI}

SUNRAYS

The *Sunrays* tool is a fun way to add beams of light to a photograph. To get started, first move the **Amount** slider to the right and you will begin to see the sunrays appear in your image. Then, click the **Place Sun Center** button and drag the white dot in your image. This is where the sunrays will originate from. I prefer to find an open spot of light to mimic the sun filtering from behind other image elements. you can also drag the sun center off of the image so that the rays emanate from outside the frame (this is my preferred method for a realistic effect).

After you have added the basic amount and relocated the sun center, you can use the following settings to further enhance the look of the rays in your scene:

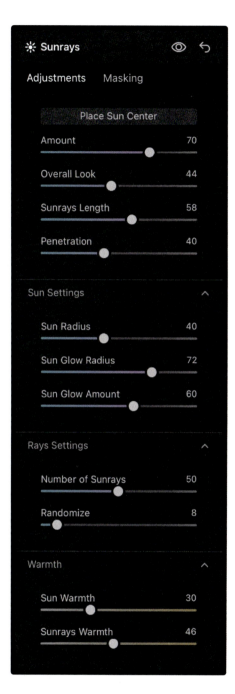

- **Amount**: Increase or decrease the overall visible effect of the *Sunrays* tool.
- **Overall Look**: The further this slider is set to the left, the more intense the contrast will be between the rays of light and your image.
- **Sunrays Length**: Changes how long the rays emanate from the sun.
- **Sun Settings**: These sliders will change how the actual sun spot looks in your photo. Use the **Sun Radius** slider to make the size of the sun larger or smaller, and use the **Sun Glow Radius** to increase the soft glow of light surrounding the sun. The **Sun Glow Amount** slider determines how intense the glow will be.
- **Rays Settings**: Increase the **Number of Sunrays** slider to add more beams of light (or reduce it to zero for a softer effect). You can also play with the **Randomize** slider to alter how the rays appear.
- **Warmth**: Intensify the warmth of the sun and sun rays. For a more realistic effect, keep these settings to a lower number (under 50).

Before

After Sunrays

Before

After Sunrays

DRAMATIC

The *Dramatic* adjustment does two main things: It decreases saturation and adds contrast. It's a nice enhancement to photos that you want to look gritty or grungy. Start by increasing the **Amount** slider, which will immediately give your image the desired effect. Then, increase or decrease the **Local Contrast** slider to change the intensity of the contrast. Lastly, you can use the **Brightness** and **Saturation** sliders to further stylize the look.

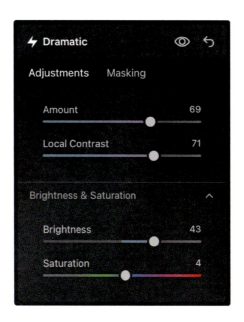

Before

After Dramatic

MOOD

The *Mood* tool allows you to colorize your photographs using Lookup Tables (LUT files). LUTs are essentially presets that contain both color and tonal data and can be used in many applications, which makes them extremely versatile. To get started, first click the **Choose LUT** drop down and select a preset from the list. After applying the preset you can further customize the look by setting the **Amount**, **Contrast**, and **Saturation** of the added style.

Luminar Neo includes a good selection of default LUTs, and you can also load your own custom LUT file if you have some favorites you have downloaded or created yourself. To add these to the Luminar Neo drop-down list, click the **Choose LUT** drop down and select *Add Custom LUT files*. Navigate to the LUT files on your computer (they will typically be in the .CUBE file type). Once installed they will appear in the *Custom LUTs* category in the drop-down list.

Before

After Mood

TONING

The *Toning* adjustment is a great way to give your image a cross-processed or colorized effect. You can go as subtle or extreme as you like with this tool, and it can also give your photo an old-school film look as well.

To get started, choose whether you first want to adjust the **Shadows** or **Highlights**. Next, increase the **Saturation** slider, which will help you to see the effect start to take hold. Then, adjust the **Hue**, which allows you to choose the color. The **Balance** slider at the bottom of the panel lets you shift which color is more prominent. I tend to prefer a teal (shadows) and orange (highlights) split-toning effect with my images, adding a classic colorized effect that works on many types of photographs.

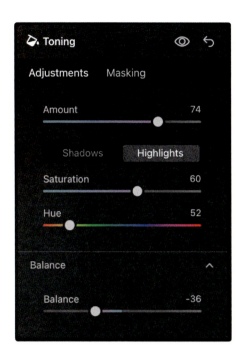

Before

After Toning

Chapter 4: Adjustments 73

MATTE

The *Matte* adjustment is a stylistic effect that essentially reduces contrast and adds a haze over the image. It's a trendy look that can work on a wide variety of images. By increasing the **Amount** slider you will begin to see the effect: Black areas will become hazy and soft, and contrast will be reduced. Adjust the Fade slider to further soften the blacks, and increase both the **Contrast** and **Vividness** sliders for a more custom look.

In the *Color Toning* section, you can also add a color tone to the photo, which will be most noticeable in the blacks and shadow areas. Begin by moving the **Range** slider to the right, which will act similarly to an "amount" slider for the colorized effect. Then, use the **Hue** slider to choose your color, and increase or decrease the intensity of the color with the **Saturation** slider at the bottom.

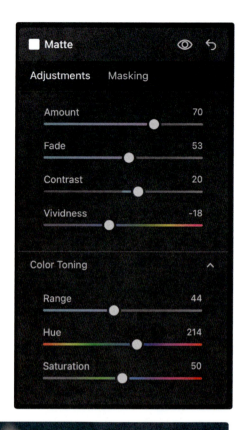

Before   After Matte

MYSTICAL

The *Mystical* adjustment will add a glowing and ethereal look to your photos, similar to a darker "fantasy" style. I particularly enjoy using it on forest and waterfall photographs; it reminds me of a fairy-tale! But it can be used on a wide variety of images, as well. It's a good "finishing touch" for many images when you want to add a touch of darker contrast and saturation.

- **Amount**: Increase or decrease the intensity of the effect.
- **Shadows**: Add brightness to the dark areas.
- **Smoothness**: Increasing this slider will feather the edge of the glowing areas with the rest of the photo, while reducing it will make the transition more harsh.
- **Colorize**: Use the **Saturation** and **Warmth** sliders to intensify or subdue the color in the image. I find adding a touch of warmth helps with the overall look for most images.

Before

After Mystical

Chapter 4: Adjustments

GLOW

The *Glow* adjustment adds a bright glow to the light and white parts of an image, and is a good fit for photographs with water (waterfalls, crashing waves, etc.), or even portraits. Once you set the **Amount** slider you can also play around with the different **Type** settings.

- **Amount**: Move this slider to the right to see the effect. A higher setting will add more glow to your image.
- **Type**: The default is *Soft Focus Bright*, which is a good option for most images when adding glow. But in some cases it might be a bit too powerful. I tend to prefer the *Orton Effect* style, which tends to balance the overall effect quite well. The *Glow* setting is the most subdued (it will primarily affect only the bright areas of the scene), and Orton Soft style will create a soft and bright glow throughout the image.
- **Softness**: Softens the glow effect and helps it transition with the non-glowy parts of the image.
- **Brightness**: Increase or decrease the amount of brightness of the glow effect.
- **Contrast**: Increase or decrease the amount of contrast of the glow effect.
- **Warmth**: Increase or decrease the warmth of the glow in the scene.

Before   After Glow

FILM GRAIN

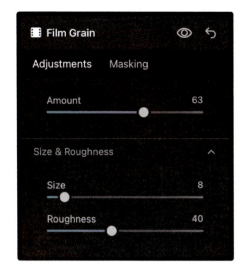

The *Film Grain* adjustment in Luminar Neo is fairly straightforward: Increase the **Amount** slider to add grain. There are also options for setting the tool's **Size** and **Roughness** to customize your film grain look.

This is a good tool to use if you want to replicate an old-school film look by easily adding film grain. Another good use is when you are replacing a sky or doing any other type of composite work. Adding film grain to the photo helps make the image look more realistic and "blends" the layers together. All images have some noise in them, but when you put two different photographs together they don't always have the same quality and size of noise. Adding film grain helps to disguise the original noise and makes it appear as if all elements of the composite came from the same photograph.

Before

After Film Grain (zoomed-in to show details)

PORTRAIT TOOLS

The *Portrait* tools in Luminar Neo work quickly to create beautiful effects with only a few adjustments. Whether you want to blur the background or clean up skin blemishes, you'll find a wonderful assortment of tools at your fingertips.

PORTRAIT BOKEH AI

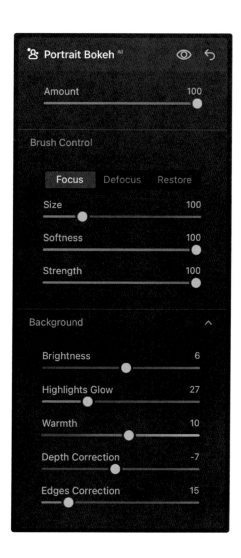

This tool works by using AI to recognize a person in a photo, and then will add photo-realistic lens blur to the background. It essentially creates an automatic mask of the person while adding a front-to-back lens blur effect to the rest of the scene. This tool will only be editable when Luminar can find a person in the image.

- **Amount**: This sets the overall effect amount.
- **Brush Control**: Sometimes the tool won't get everything perfect on the first go. That's what the *Brush Control* section is for. Use the toggles — **Focus** (reveals the original image), **Defocus** (adds blur), and **Restore** (restore a previous brush stroke) — to fine-tune the adjustment. The **Size**, **Softness**, and **Strength** (Opacity) sliders allow you to change the brush to work best with the area you want to adjust.
- **Background adjustments**: Once you have your blur created, you may also want to make some adjustments to the background to help it blend better with your main subject:
    - → **Brightness**: Increase or decrease the brightness of the background.
    - → **Highlights Glow**: Intensify the glowing effect of any large spots of lights (light bulbs, candles, etc.).
    - → **Warmth**: Increase or decrease the warmth of the background.
    - → **Depth Correction**: Moves the starting point of the blur to ensure that the focal planes of your subject and background are aligned.
    - → **Edges Correction**: Cleans up the edges of the mask.

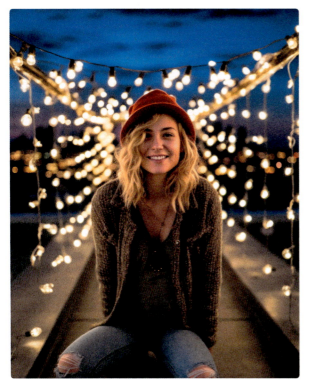

Before

After Portrait Bokeh^{AI}

Before

After Portrait Bokeh^{AI}

Chapter 4: Adjustments   **79**

FACE ᴬᴵ

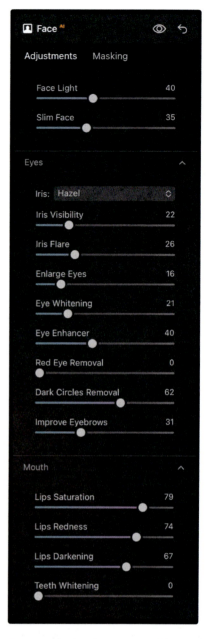

Fine-tune your portraits with simple adjustments in the *Face*^{AI} tool. This tool is organized into three sections with multiple sliders to help stylize and perfect the faces in your images, and it works on individual and group photos.

- **Face Light**: Increase the brightness to the face, acting as a subtle spotlight to help make the faces in the image stand out.
- **Slim Face**: Gently slim the face shape.
- **Eyes**: Change the color of the iris, add a catch-light with the <u>Iris Flare</u> slider, and make other adjustments to the eye area of people in your photos. You can also remove red-eye if it is present in your image. *Tip: Use a low setting when applying the <u>Eye Whitening</u> slider to prevent the eyes from looking unrealistic.*
- **Mouth**: Enhance the lips by adding saturation, reducing brightness, and making them more red. You can also make the teeth whiter (go light with this setting to keep the image realistic-looking). *Tip: Use the Masking brush in this tool to remove lip effects to people who you do not want to make the lips more saturated or darker.*

Before

After Face^{AI}

SKIN AI

This tool will help clean up blemishes on the skin. Use the **Amount** slider to set the overall amount of smoothing, and the **Shine Removal** slider for any bright glare on the face. You can also check the **Skin Defects Removal** AI box to automatically remove blemishes. *Tip: Use this tool multiple times on the same photo when you have a face with many blemishes.*

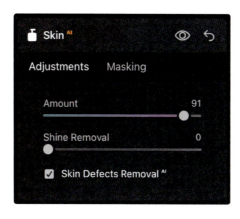

Before

After Skin AI (used twice)

FAVORITE EDITING TOOLS

If discover that you are using some of the same tools over and over, you can add them as **Favorites** for easy access. Right-click over a of the tool panel name and choose "Add to Favorites" and the tool will move to a new **Favorites** section will appear near the top of the Tools panel.

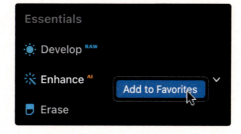

Chapter 4: Adjustments

BODY^{AI}

This tool will help adjust the shape of a person's overall body, as well as "pinch in" the abdomen area. It can be a helpful tool to use for baggy clothing that hides a person's true shape.

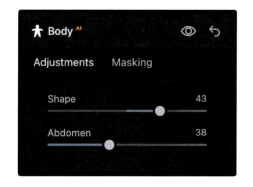

- **Shape**: Move this slider to the left to expand the shape, and move it to the right to slim the shape.
- **Abdomen**: Increase this slider to "pinch in" the abdomen area of the body.

Before

After Body^{AI}

HIGH KEY

A photograph that is "high key" means that it is bright with very little shadow detail, and oftentimes this term refers to something bright photographed against a light or white background (such as a white rose in the snow). In Luminar, the *High Key* replicates that bright, overexposed look by adding a desaturated, bright, and somewhat washed-out effect. While this look works well for portraits, it can also be applied to other image types.

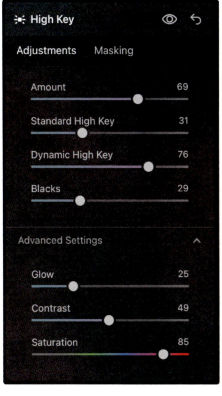

- **Amount**: Increase this slider to see this adjustment take effect. This is similar to an intensity setting for all other sliders in this tool.
- **Standard High Key**: Increases the standard high-key effect.
- **Dynamic High Key**: This slider is best for portraits, as it adds the high-key effect while also considering skin tones.
- **Blacks**: Moving this slider to the right will help bring detail back in the darkest areas of the image.
- **Glow**: Adds a subtle glow to the bright parts of the image.
- **Contrast**: Increases overall contrast to this effect.
- **Saturation**: By default, this adjustment will default to slightly desaturating the image. Increasing this slider will restore the image's original saturation look.

Before

After High Key

Chapter 4: Adjustments 83

PROFESSIONAL TOOLS

The *Professional* tools cater to the exacting demands of experienced and selective users. Discover these exceptional tools in Luminar, which enable superior control over color and tone, and elevate your editing experience.

SUPERCONTRAST

The *Supercontrast* tool lets you fine-tune the contrast in your image by targeting either the **Highlights**, **Midtones**, and **Shadows**. Each *Contrast* slider will *increase the amount of contrast* to the specific region you selected. The *Balance* sliders change the balance of this contrast setting.

To break it down even further, I like to think of each *Contrast* slider as an "amount" slider, allowing me to determine how much contrast I want in each region (highlights, midtones, and shadows). After this slider is set, by moving *Balance* sliders to the right it will make that region darker, and moving it to the left makes the targeted region darker.

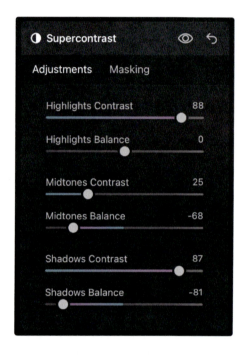

Before

After Supercontrast

COLOR HARMONY

This tool is perfect for advanced and precise color editing in your images.

- **Brilliance**: Increases the intensity of the colors in your image. Similar to a "saturation" slider.
- **Warmth**: Increase or decrease the warmth in the entire image.
- **Color Contrast**: Changes the brightness and contrast in specific color groups. Use the **Amount** slider to set the intensity, and adjust the **Hue** slider while watching your image to see the results. *Tip: Keep this adjustment to around a setting of 30 or lower to prevent over-processed results.*
- **Split Color Warmth**: Targets the warm and cool sections in your photo by allowing you to increase or decrease the warmth in each of these areas independent of the other.
- **Color Balance**: Targeted color adjustments to the shadows, midtones, and highlights.

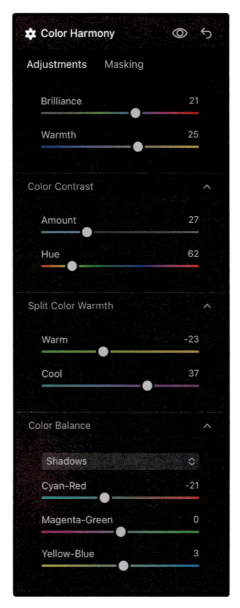

Before

After Color Harmony

Chapter 4: Adjustments   85

DODGE & BURN

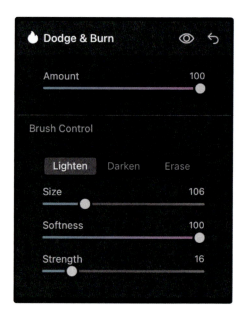

The *Dodge & Burn* tool is an incredibly effective way to "sculpt" a photograph by painting in shadows and highlights. To begin adding this effect, select either the **Lighten** or **Darken** options and begin painting over your image. I recommend setting the *Brush Control's* **Strength** slider to 10% or 20% to prevent overdoing the effect, and if you need more intensity, paint several brush strokes over the same area. Then, play with the **Amount** slider after you've made your edits, just in case the result is overpowering.

Another good rule of thumb when painting is to use the **Lighten** brush on areas that are already bright, and use the **Darken** brush on areas that are already dark. This will allow you to fully control the amount of contrast and intensity you are adding to your photo.

Before

After Dodge & Burn

CLONE

The *Clone* tool allows you to remove unwanted areas from your image by cloning from other parts of your photo. This differs from the *Erase* tool in that it gives you much more precise control over what is being removed, as well as what part of the image is replacing it. You may find this tool ideal when you have straight lines in your photo with a blemish or an object you wish to remove. You'll be able to manually correct the blemish and also keep the lines straight by properly aligning the source area with your brush strokes.

After activating this tool, click in your image to set the original source (the area you want to use to cover up the blemish in your photo). After you set the source, anywhere you paint with the brush will originate from this source, and then the rest of the brush strokes will map to other areas based on the original source selection. To change the source location, press and hold the **OPT** (macOS) or **ALT** (Windows) key and click. You can do this as many times as you like during the same cloning process. Use the settings in the panel to set the **Size**, **Softness**, and **Strength** of the brush as you paint over the image.

Before

After Clone

Chapter 4: Adjustments

EXTENSIONS

5

Luminar Neo offers add-on extensions to further expand the power of your editing workflow. These are optional and do not come pre-installed with the basic Luminar Neo software purchase. You can purchase and install the extensions by clicking the **Extras** button at the top of the Luminar Neo application window.

HDR MERGE

HDR — or, high dynamic range — is a type of photography where you create multiple photos of the same scene at different exposures. Then, you blend the images together using software to get the highest range of tones in the photo. Photos where this may be warranted are any high-contrast scene where setting the exposure for one area will mean that you lose detail in another area , either because it is too bright or too dark. One example would be photographing a sunset (the sky is bright, but the landscape may be dark) or the interior of a building with windows (the outside light through the window is much brighter than the interior lights of the interior room).

Luminar Neo has an extension that will blend your HDR images together to create a single file. In fact, it will even work with one image to bring out as much tonal detail as possible! In the step-by-step example on the next page, I have seven images I photographed of the inside of an abandoned building, and I collected them into an Album in the *Catalog* module. Let's walk through the process of converting these five images into a final HDR image to discover how it works.

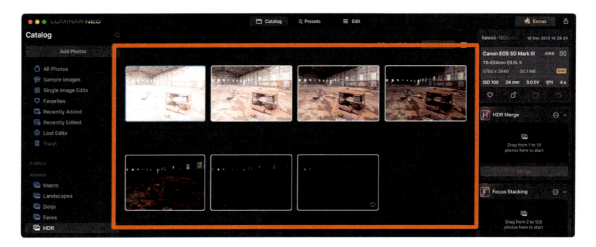

1. **Drag the files to the extension**: The first step is to select (highlight) all of the images you want to work with in the Grid view. In this example, I have the seven images of the abandoned building. Drag all of your selected images over the *HDR Merge* extension on the right.

2. **Adjust settings**: Click the ellipsis icon on the upper-right part of this extension panel to open the *Settings*:

   → **Auto Alignment**: Check this setting if you did not use a tripod for your bracketed exposures to help align the images.

   → **Chromatic Aberration Reduction**: This will help remove any purple or green fringing around subjects that is sometimes visible on brighter images.

   → **Ghost Reduction**: If you have a photo with moving objects (trees, water, people, etc.), you may want to check this box and then choose a reference image. This will help eliminate any "ghosts" that appear from movement between frames.

3. **Merge the images**: When ready, click the **Merge** button to create the merged HDR image. Once processing is completed, a new folder appears in the Folders section on the left called *HDR Merge*. This is where all images created using the HDR Merge extension will be saved. Now you are free to edit the merged HDR in the Edit module to customize the look of the image.

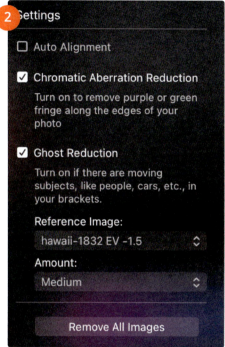
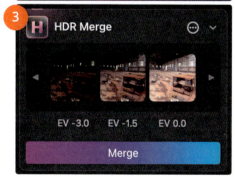

Before & After (HDR Merge)

Chapter 5: Extensions

FOCUS STACKING

Focus stacking is a method of creating multiple frames of the same image, with each frame photographed at different focal planes. This is typically done by positioning a camera on a tripod and changing the focus a small amount each frame, and is common with macro photography where it is difficult to create one image with the entire subject in focus. You can use the *Focus Stacking* extension in Luminar Neo to automatically merge these frames together. Here's how:

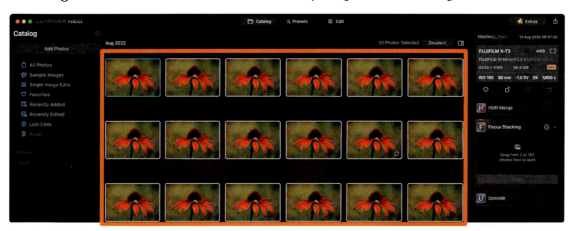

1. **Drag the files to the extension**: In the Catalog module, select and highlight the images you want to stack. In this example, I have 11 images of a spider on a flower.

2. **Adjust settings**: Click the ellipsis icon on the upper-right part of this extension panel to open the *Settings*:

   → **Auto Alignment**: It's a good idea to have this checked, just in case there was movement between frames.

   → **Chromatic Aberration Reduction**: This will help remove any purple or green fringing around subjects that is sometimes visible on brighter images.

3. **Stack the images**: Click the **Stack** button to process the images and blend them together, creating a photo that has a much deeper depth of field. Focus-stacked images will automatically appear in the *Focus Stacking* folder on the left in the *Catalog* module.

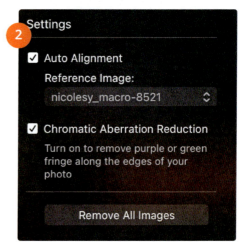

Before (zoomed in)

After Focus Stacking extension (zoomed in). Notice how there is more detail on the spider's body and legs than is visible in the "before" image.

Chapter 5: Extensions 91

UPSCALE^{AI}

The *Upscale*^{AI} extension will upscale your images up to 6x their original size while preserving details. This is a great feature to use when you have a small photo that you want enlarged, or perhaps you cropped in a photo quite a bit and want to return it to the original dimensions.

To use this feature, access the *Catalog* module and drag a photo over the Upscale extension panel. Then, choose the amount you wish to enlarge it (2x, 4x, or 6x) (**A**). The extension also has an option in the *Settings* called **Face Enhancer** (**B**) to use with images of people (click the gear icon to view this option). This pop up also has some more useful information about the extension, including the minimum image size you an start with and the maximum output size possible.

In the example below, the original image (input = 2000 px by 1339 px) to **4x the original size** (output = 8000 px by 5356 px). The example areas are zoomed so you can see the comparison between the smaller image and its upscaled counterpart.

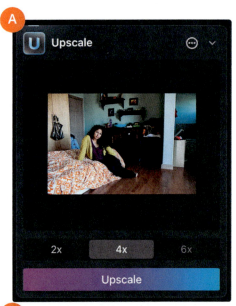

Before (1000 px by 1339 px)

After Upscale^{AI} *(4x output = 8000 px by 5356 px)*

NOISELESS ^{AI}

The *Noiseless*^{AI} tool in the *Edit* module helps to remove grain and noise from images. It is superior to the Denoise tool because it uses AI to ensure that the quality of the photo is maintained, and offers advanced sliders to help perfect the balance of noise reduction and detail enhancement.

To get started with this extension, make sure you are in the *Edit* module. The Noiseless^{AI} tool is located at the top of the tools on the right. You'll notice right away that the tool offers a suggested initial adjustment for the photo you are working on. In this example, it suggests I use the **High** setting.

Once you click the initial button (Low, Middle, or High), the sliders will activate below. These settings can be fine-tuned to remove the noise from your image while preserving details and sharpness:

- **Luminosity Denoise**: Further removes noise and grain. *Be cautious with this slider so you don't over-smooth your image or remove too many fine details.*
- **Details**: Helps restore fine details in the image. *Using this too heavily can introduce noise or artifacts in your photo.*
- **Sharpness**: Brings sharpness back to the edges of objects in your images. *If used too aggressively it can introduce halos and unnatural "crunchy" edges.*

Before (zoomed in)

After Noiseless^{AI} (zoomed in)

Chapter 5: Extensions   93

SUPERSHARP AI

When you want to correct a blurry photo in Luminar, **Supersharp** AI is a great tool for the job. This tool uses AI to analyze the content and sharpen the areas that should be sharp and really shines when your photo has a touch of motion blur in it (such as hand movement, trees blowing in the breeze, etc.). While it's not possible to perfectly sharpen a blurry image, this tool does a great job of bringing out details and can easily save a photo from ending up in the reject pile.

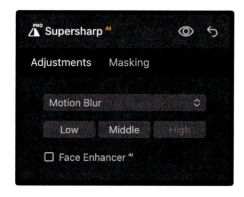

- **Universal**: Use this setting from the drop down for standard images (no motion blur).
- **Motion Blur**: When there is motion blur or camera shake in your photo, choose this setting to help bring details back to the blurry areas.
- **Strength settings**: Choose either Low, Middle, or High settings.
- **Face Enhancer** AI: Helps to improve and enhance details in the face.

Before (zoomed in)

After Supersharp AI (zoomed in)

MAGIC LIGHT ^AI

Magic Light ^AI is a fun extension that works to stylize and enhance light sources in your photos.

Note: This tool will be editable only when working on images that have light sources in them, such as candles, street lamps, and holiday lights. If your photo does not have this type of element in the scene, the Edit panel will be grayed out and the sliders will not function.

- **Intensity**: Similar to an "amount" setting for the overall effect.
- **Size**: Increases the size of the beam and glow effects.
- **Beam Width**: Sets the width of each individual beam. The wider the beam is, the softer its edges will become.
- **Glow**: Sets the glowiness of the light source(s).
- **Clearness**: A higher setting will make the beams more "crisp," whereas a lower setting will make the beams more blurred and softer.
- **Brightness**: Intensifies the brightness of the beam effect.
- **Number of Beams**: Sets the number of beams emanating from each light source.
- **Rotation**: Rotates the beams.

Before (zoomed in)

After Magic Light ^AI *(zoomed in)*

Chapter 5: Extensions

BACKGROUND REMOVAL ^AI

The **Background Removal**^AI tool allows you to quickly remove the background from any photo. To access this tool, make sure you are in the Edit module and have the layer you want to use selected, and then access the **Layer Properties** panel. Access the **Masking** section of this panel, and then click **Background Removal**^AI.

As with any post-processing method, the clearer your photo is and the more distinct the subject is from its background, the better this tool will work. If your image is busy, has too much blur (bokeh), or there is not enough contrast between the object you want to mask and the background you wish to remove, then it may have a difficult time working properly.

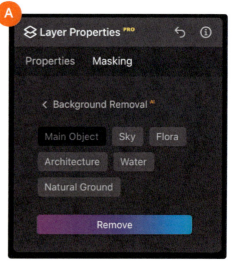

In this example, I would like to place the hot air balloon on a new background. I start by opening the hot air balloon photo, go to the Layer Properties, and access the Maskings section (**A**). Then I click **Background Removal**^AI. Luminar Neo finds the balloon and highlights it in red, letting me know that it will keep that part of the photo and remove (mask out) the rest (**B**). It also shows me other options to add to my mask, so if I wanted to keep those areas in the photo, I would click each option and the mask would update.

Once I'm ready, I click **Remove** to mask out the background (**C**). It looks like there are a few spots that need to be masked back in on the mask, and because masks are editable, I can brush those areas back in at any time.

Before   *After Background Removal*^AI

Next, I need to add my new background. In the **Layers** panel on the left, I click the **+** icon, choose **Load Image** at the top, and then navigate to a photo of a tulip field and select it from the thumbnail list once it appears. This puts the new image on the top layer, so I click and drag the tulip field layer so that it is below the masked layer of the hot air balloon. With the tulip field layer still selected, I go to the **Layer Properties** panel and set the **Opacity** to *100* (**D**).

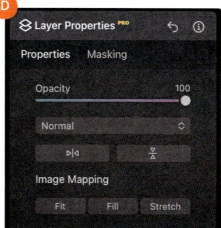

The balloon needs to be resized and positioned, so I go to the Layers panel, click the layer to activate it, and make sure that the **Layer Properties** panel is also active. Next, I use the transform controls to resize and reposition the balloon so it is in the background. Then, I access the **Mask** section within the **Layer Properties** panel (**E**), select the Brush tool and brush in some of the small gaps that were missed from the original ***Background Removal*** ^{AI} mask. Lastly, I go back to the Properties section and change the blend mode to Multiply to help the image blend better with its new background (**F**).

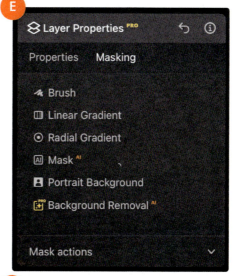

Chapter 5: Extensions 97

PANORAMA STITCHING

The *Panorama Stitching* tool allows you to create a panorama image from a series of photographs, HDR brackets, or even a video. This extension works the same way as the other extensions by dragging photos or a video over the tool and then adjusting your settings. Let's take a look at how to use this feature, along with some general tips on creating images and videos for a panorama photograph.

PHOTOGRAPHY TIPS

There are some general guidelines you should follow when photographing your images and videos to merge into a panorama in Luminar Neo. First, it's best if you photograph each frame *vertically* for horizontal panoramas and *horizontally* for vertical panoramas. This ensures that you get the most all-around space in your frame possible. Next, when creating a still photograph, try to *overlap each frame by about 20%* to make sure that the images will have enough image data to stitch together seamlessly. And lastly, if using a tripod, make sure that your *camera is properly leveled* throughout the entire length of your panorama so you have a beautifully-leveled image after you merge them all together (not having leveled frames could result in cropping out too much of your photograph).

The images below show an example of a four-frame vertical panorama with plenty of overlap to assist with stitching the photos.

BASIC & HDR PANORAMA STITCHING

Luminar Neo can create panoramas from both a basic set of panorama frames (similar to the example images on the previous page), or from multiple bracketed frames to create an HDR panorama. When creating HDR frames for a panorama, you would use your exposure bracketing settings on your camera for each shot of the panorama to create multiple exposures of each frame. You can then use all of these images in the Panorama Stitching tool, which will automatically do the HDR merging and panorama stitching at the same time.

Here's how to create a panorama in Luminar Neo:

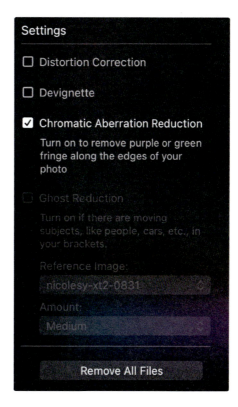

1. **Drag the files to the extension**: In the Catalog module, select all images you want to add to your panorama. You an do this by clicking the first image, then hold the **SHIFT** key and click the last image. Then, drag the images over the Panorama Stitching extension on the right.

2. **Adjust settings as needed**: Click the ellipsis icon on the upper-right part of this extension panel to open the *Settings*:

    → **Distortion correction**: This heps to reduce distortion with wide-angle photos.

    → **Devignette**: Helps remove vignetting on individual image frames that could add unwanted tonal distortions in the final merged panorama.

→ **Chromatic Aberration Reduction**: This will help remove any purple or green fringing around subjects that is sometimes visible on brighter images.

→ **Ghost Reduction**: If you are merging and HDR panorama and have a photo with moving objects (trees, water, people, etc.), you may want to check this box and then choose a reference image. This will help eliminate any "ghosts" that appear from movement between frames.

3. **Choose your projection mode**: Click the **Start** button to open the Panorama Stitching preview window. Once the images process and you can see your image, you can adjust settings to create the projection mode that suits your photo best. The descriptions below will explain why you might want to use each of the options, but it's best to click through them to visually determine which setting works best for your scene.

→ **Spherical**: Use this option when you want your panorama to cover a wide area, like a complete 360-degree scene.

→ **Cylindrical**: This is great for wide, but not very tall, panoramas as it "wraps" your images onto a flat cylinder shape, reducing distortion at the top and bottom.

→ **Mercator**: Choose this when you want to maintain the angles and shapes in your photos; just be aware it can stretch things vertically, making it ideal for less wide, more vertical scenes.

- → ⊕ **Plane**: Perfect for wide landscapes or cityscapes, this option stretches your images flat, but distortion can occur if your panorama is too tall.

- → ◎ **Fisheye**: Go for this when you want a unique, circular perspective; it distorts your panorama like you're looking through a flat fish-eye lens, adding an artistic twist.

4. **Reposition and rotate the image**: If the image positioning needs adjusting, you can click and drag within the preview window to reposition the panorama. You can also rotate the image to level the horizon by hovering over the right side of the preview window until the icon changes into a curved double arrow. Then, move the cursor up or down to rotate the image.

5. **Create the final merged photo**: When you are ready, click **Continue**. Adjust the crop as needed, and when you are ready, click the **Crop** button. Next, click **Save** and your final panorama photo will be saved in the *Panorama Stitching* folder.

VIDEO PANORAMA STITCHING

One of the really exciting features of the new Panorama Stitching extension is the ability to create a panorama image from a video. By recording a video from *side to side* or *top to bottom*, you can create the frames needed for Luminar Neo to stitch together as a classic panorama photograph. Another feature of Luminar Neo is the ability to create *action panoramas* from a video. In addition to creating the classic high-resolution image you're used to, it also takes moving elements from within the video and places them multiple times across the scene into a single still photograph.

BASIC PANORAMA FROM A VIDEO

When video is a better option for you to capture a scene, this option in Luminar is a good fit and still allows you to create a beautiful panorama photograph. Create your video from side-to-side vertically (or up-and-down horizontally) just as you would set up and photograph for still panorama frames you wish to merge. Try to keep the camera level throughout the entire sweep of your camera.

Here's how to create a *simple panorama photo* from a video file. In this example, I created a vertical video outside my front yard, moving the camera from left to right as I recorded.

1. **Drag the video file to the extension**: In the Catalog module, drag the video file over the Panorama Stitching extension. Click **Start** to begin the process.

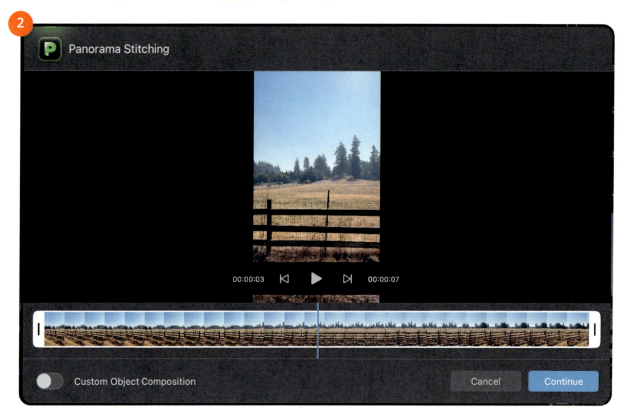

2. **Select the video area you want to use**: Luminar Neo allows you to merge up to one-minute of video. If your video is longer than one minute, you will need to select the one-minute (or less) portion of the video you want to use. Use the left and right toggles in the timeline to trim the length to the part you want to use. Click **Continue** when you are finished.

3. **Merge the images**: Once the images process and you can see your image, you can adjust settings to create the projection mode that suits your photo best, just as you would a panorama created from still images. (*See Steps 3 through 5 starting on page 100 to continue merging your panorama*).

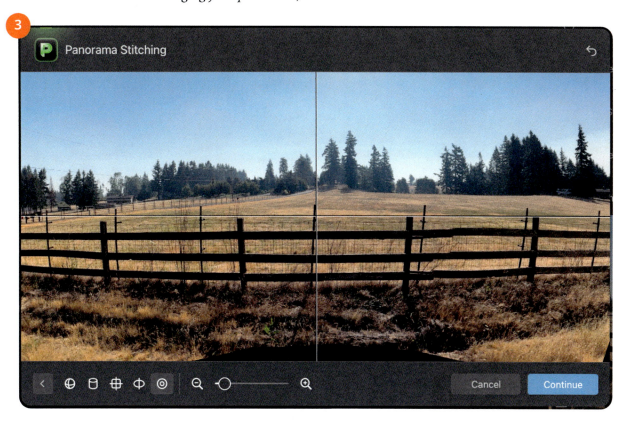

ACTION PANORAMA FROM A VIDEO

Action panoramas allow you to record a video scene with a moving object within the scene, and then Luminar Neo allows you to place the same object multiple times within the frame. The best way to set up for these types of panoramas is to create a video with a moving camera while following an object from side to side. When moving the camera, try to keep it leveled horizontally as much as possible and prevent moving the camera up or down. This will help to maintain a leveled horizontal in your photo, as well as prevent the panorama from becoming too skinny and potentially cropping out relevant image areas. *Note: You must move the camera when creating an action panorama for the stitching process to work properly.*

Here's how to create an *action panorama photo* from a video file:

1. **Drag the video file to the extension**: In the Catalog module, drag the video file over the Panorama Stitching extension (**A**). Click **Start** to begin the process.

2. **Select the video area you want to use**: Luminar Neo allows you to merge up to one-minute of video. If your video is longer than one minute, you will need to select the one-minute (or less) portion of the video you want to use. Use the left and right toggles in the timeline to trim the length to the part you want to use.

3. **Choose the object you want to replicate across the panorama**: Click the **Custom Object Composition** toggle on the bottom left and you'll notice a slight change to the timeline and video preview. Now, scroll the play-head to the point of the video where you want the subject to repeat across the panorama. For each frame you want to add, click the small blue plus icon below the timeline, and use the rectangle box in the preview to select the subject. Do this for each instance of the subject that you want repeated in the panorama. Click **Continue** when you are finished.

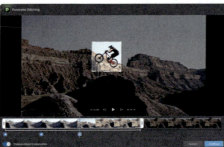

4. **Merge and crop the image**: Once the images process and you can see your image, you can adjust settings to create the projection mode that suits your photo best. (*See "Step 3" on page 100 to learn about each panorama projection mode*). When you are finished, click **Continue** to continue to the next step.

5. **Crop and save the final panorama image**. A crop preview will appear over your image. Set the crop to your liking, and then click the **Crop** button. In the final window, click **Save** and your final panorama photo will be saved in the ***Panorama Stitching*** folder.

Chapter 5: Extensions   105

FINAL TOUCHES   6

Luminar Neo has a few more functions that you may find useful in your everyday work. These include using the software as a plugin from Adobe® Lightroom® Classic, Adobe® Photoshop®, and Apple Photos for macOS, along with batch-processing multiple images at once, and finally, exporting your work to share online or print.

USING LUMINAR AS A PLUGIN

For photographers who have multiple editing apps at their disposal, the plugin option for Luminar Neo is a great fit. This option allows you to work with an image first in either Adobe® Lightroom® Classic or Photoshop®, and then edit the photo in Luminar Neo without having to first export a photo to your computer. And, if you use the Apple Photos app, you can benefit from the addition of Luminar Neo as well. *Note: Some extensions are not available when using Luminar Neo as a plugin from other apps.*

INSTALLING THE LUMINAR PLUGIN

To use these plugins, you first need to install them. Here's how to install the plugin into Lightroom and Photoshop.

1. Quit all programs you want to install plugin into.
2. Open Luminar Neo, click the **Luminar Neo menu** on the top-left of the application window, and select **Install Plugins**.
3. Click the **Install** button next to the program you want to use. You may also uninstall plugins using this menu.

To use Luminar Neo with the **Apple Photos** app, please see "Apple Photos" on page 110.

A NOTE FOR WINDOWS USERS

You will need to run Luminar Neo as an administrator when installing plugins. To do this, right-click the Luminar Neo icon and select **Run as administrator**.

ADOBE LIGHTROOM CLASSIC

Adobe Lightroom Classic is a fantastic tool for organizing and editing your images. In fact, it's my preference for all of my images when importing, organizing, editing, and even exporting my work. And, when I want to benefit from Luminar Neo's editing capabilities, I can easily jump back into Luminar to add finishing touches to my images. Here's how you can use Luminar Neo as a plugin from Lightroom Classic:

1. First, edit your photo in Lightroom Classic using the Develop module. You will want to make sure that all raw edits are properly adjusted before bringing the image into Luminar Neo.

2. With the photo selected, go to **Photo > Edit In > Luminar Neo**.

3. In the pop-up window, choose **Edit a Copy with Lightroom Adjustments**. You can also click **Copy File Options** to change the default file type. Then, click **Edit**.

4. The image will open into Luminar Neo. Then, add your finishing touches: Apply a preset or use the **Edit** module for adjustments and enhancements.

5. After making your adjustments, click **Apply** on the top right to bring the photo back to Lightroom. *Note: Adjustments and tools applied in Luminar as a plugin from Lightroom Classic will be flattened (tools and adjustments applied will no longer be editable once the file is back in Lightroom).*

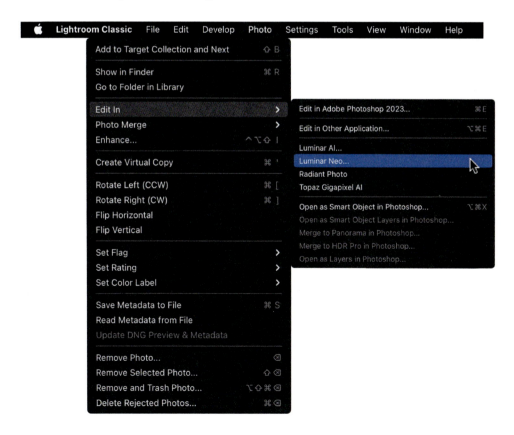

ADOBE PHOTOSHOP

Adobe Photoshop has a great amount of flexibility when working with Luminar Neo. When you pair editing with layers in Photoshop, you are able to maximize your potential for creativity and re-editability with your documents. In this section, I'll demonstrate the most efficient workflow when using Photoshop and Luminar Neo together using Smart Objects.

1. **Begin with a photo opened up into Photoshop**: This could be a raw image that you edited using Camera Raw and you're ready to make stylized adjustments to, or perhaps you have a layered document and you want to take advantage of Luminar's filters or extensions as a finishing touch.

2. **Make sure the Layers panel is visible**: If you don't see the Layers panel, go to *Window > Layers* to make it visible.

   → If you have only one layer in your document, duplicate the layer. You can do this quickly by selecting the layer and using the keyboard shortcut **COMMAND + J** (macOS) or **CTRL + J** (Windows).

   → If your document has multiple layers, activate the top-most active layer. Then, use the keyboard shortcut **COMMAND + OPT + SHIFT + E** (macOS) or **CTRL + ALT + SHIFT + E** (Windows). This will create a new merged layer and place it above the active layer.

3. **Create a Smart Object (optional)**: Select your newly duplicated or merged layer, and go to *Layer > Smart Objects > Convert to Smart Objects*.

4. **Edit the layer in Luminar Neo**: Make sure that the Smart Object layer is active. Then, go to *Filter > Skylum Software > Luminar Neo*. Edit the image in Luminar by applying presets and/or Edit tools. When you're finished, click **Apply** and the edits will be applied, Luminar Neo will close, and you'll see the changes appear in Photoshop.

THE ADVANTAGES OF PHOTOSHOP SMART OBJECTS

If you want to retain your edits and work non-destructively in Photoshop, you'll likely want to take advantage of Smart Objects. There are many reasons you would want to use Smart Objects, and below I've listed out how they are helpful when working with the Luminar Neo plugin:

- **Non-destructive filter application**: Applying filters from external plugins like Luminar Neo to Smart Objects allows you to work non-destructively, preserving the original image data and ensuring that your filter adjustments can be reversed or modified at any time. This allows you to fine-tune or completely change the filter effect without having to start from scratch or redo the entire filter process on a flattened layer.

- **Filter stacking**: Working with Smart Objects enables you to stack multiple filters from external plugins or Photoshop itself, creating a unique combination of effects. You can easily rearrange or toggle the visibility of individual filters, providing more creative control over your image editing process.

- **Selective filter application**: By converting a layer to a Smart Object and applying a filter, you can create a layer mask for the Smart Filter to selectively apply the effect to specific areas of the image. This flexibility enables precise control over where the filter effect is visible, without permanently altering the underlying image.

- **Filter blending options**: When applying filters to Smart Objects, you can experiment with different blending modes and opacity settings to create a variety of visual effects, all while preserving the ability to edit or remove the filter effect.

LIGHTROOM CLASSIC + PHOTOSHOP SMART OBJECTS

If you use Lightroom Classic and want to edit your images into Luminar Neo, you may also consider first opening the file into Photoshop so that you can take advantage of Smart Objects. You can even edit your file directly from Lightroom into Photoshop as a Smart Object, and then open Luminar Neo to apply your edits. To do this, in Lightroom Classic, go to *Photo > Edit In > Open as Smart Object in Photoshop*.

APPLE PHOTOS

Apple Photos for macOS allows you to use Luminar Neo as an extension. Here's how:

1. In the Apple Photos app, open an image and click **Edit** on the top-right corner.

2. Click the **Extensions** drop down (the three dots at the top) and choose Luminar Neo from the list.

3. Edit your photo in Luminar and click **Save Changes** at the top when you're done. Your photo will open up into the Photos app once again. Click **Done** in the top-right corner when you're finished with your edit.

If you don't see the Luminar Neo extension listed in the drop down (from Step 2), you'll need to open your computer's **System Settings** and follow these steps:

1. Go to **Privacy & Security**, then scroll down until you see a section called **Others**. Click the **Extensions** option from this section.

2. Click the **Photos Editing** option.

3. Scroll down until you see **Luminar Neo** in this list and make sure that there is a check next to it. The Luminar Neo extension is now installed and can now be accessed from the Apple Photos app.

EDIT ANY IMAGE FROM YOUR COMPUTER

It's not necessary to add photos to the catalog or even start from another application. In fact, you can simply drag-and-drop any image from your computer into the Luminar Neo application window and begin editing! Below I've listed out some ways to use this feature, as well as what to expect:

- **Drag-and-drop**: If you have a photo in a folder on your computer and you don't want to go through the process of adding it to the catalog (or opening it using the plugin method) then you can simply drag the file over the opened Luminar Neo application window and drop it in. Then you can use any of the Luminar Neo extensions or editing tools.

- **From the menu**: You can use the menu to open a single image. Go to *File > Edit Single Image* and navigate to the file you want to edit.

- **Single Image Edits category**: Creating an edit using one of the above methods will add it to a section called *Single Image Edits* within the catalog. The image files are still in their original folder location on your computer, but they are grouped together in a single location.

- **Moving files into the catalog**: If you have a photo in the *Single Image Edits* category but would like to move it to your catalog, you can do this by dragging and dropping the file into a folder in the Folders category.

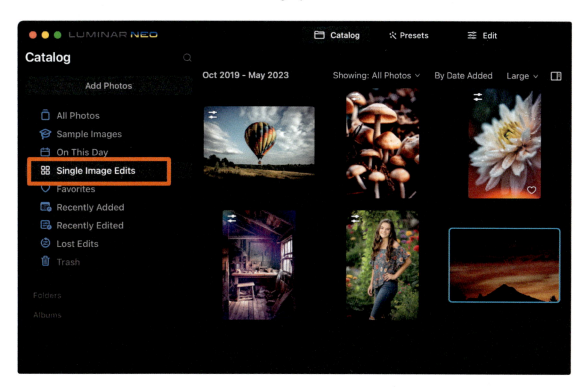

Chapter 6: Final Touches

BATCH PROCESSING

One of the fastest ways to edit a group of similar photos is to use batch processing (or, syncing image edits). This process allows you to edit one photo and then copy those edits over to other images. *Note: Syncing image edits requires that you use images from within the catalog or in the Single Image Edits folder.*

Here's how to batch-process your photos in Luminar Neo:

1. Begin by editing one photo in the *Edit* module.
2. Now, go into the *Catalog* module, view your images in Gallery mode to see all of the image thumbnails, and locate of the images you want to batch process. It is helpful if these images are in the same folder or album.
3. There are two ways that you can sync edits across images:
   → Activate the image you just edited and go to *Image > Adjustments > Copy Adjustments*. Then, select all other images you want to apply these edits to. Then, go to *Image > Adjustments > Paste Adjustments* and the edits will be copied over to all selected images.
   → Click the image you just edited to highlight it in blue. Then, press and hold the **COMMAND** (macOS) or **CTRL** (Windows) key while clicking all other images in the group you want to batch process (they will be highlighted in white). You can also hold the **SHIFT** key to select multiple images that are all next to each other in the thumbnail view. Then, go to *Image > Adjustments > Sync Adjustments* and your photos will all be processed using the same edits from the first photo.

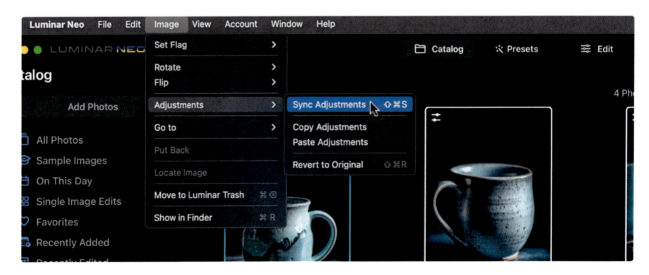

EXPORTING FROM LUMINAR NEO

Once you have a finished file inside of the standalone application, you'll want to export your image so that you print it or share it online. In this section, I'll walk through how to save the file to your computer.

To begin, you'll need to access the Export window. Click the **Export** button on the top-right of the window and select *Share to > Disk*. Alternately, from the menu you can go to *File > Export*. This can be access from any module within Luminar Neo.

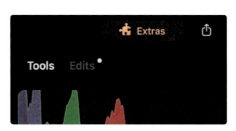

Then, choose the *location* where you want to save your file. This can be anywhere on your computer. You can also *rename* the file at this point. Before you save your exported file, you may also want to adjust some of the settings on this pop up:

- **Sharpen**: Choose how much sharpening you would like to add to your exported file. The options here are *None*, *Low*, *Medium*, and *High*.

- **Resize**: If you are printing the exported file, you'll likely want to use the *Original* option for this setting. For sharing on the web, you may want to consider scaling the file down. You can use any of the options to set how you want to do this: *Long Edge*, *Short Edge*, and *Dimensions*. The size you choose is up to you, however, I tend to keep my exported files that I share online somewhere between 2000 px and 3000 px on the long edge.

- **Color space**: Select the color space you would like to use when exporting. (For sharing online or printing, most often you will want this set to sRGB.)

- **Format**: This is where you choose the file type. The options are: *JPEG*, *PNG*, *TIFF*, *JPEG-2000*, *Photoshop*, and *PDF*.

- **Resolution**: Set the *pixels-per-inch* or *pixels-per-centimeter* for your exported file. For online sharing, use a setting of 72. For printing, 240 or 300 are good standards.

- **Quality**: Choose the quality of your export. For the best-looking file, set it to *100*. Reducing this setting will reduce the quality of your image and you will see noticeable artifacts and banding in lower-quality exports. However, reducing quality may also make the file size much smaller, so it's a compromise you may need to make if file size is important.

CONCLUSION

As we reach the end of this book on Luminar Neo, I hope you've found the journey rewarding and feel more confident in your ability to use this powerful tool. We've traveled through a wide array of features, providing you with practical knowledge to enhance your photo editing journey.

From mastering the Luminar Neo catalog to organizing your photos to experimenting with presets, you now have a broad set of tools at your disposal. We dove into the world of layers and masks, a game-changer in the editing process, and discovered how Luminar Neo can integrate with other software like Lightroom Classic, Photoshop, and Apple Photos, as well as how it can be used with individual image files.

You've learned the time-saving skill of batch-processing, a handy tool to quickly edit multiple photos. Plus, we explored the exciting new Luminar Neo extensions, which open up a world of creative possibilities.

But don't forget, the real magic of Luminar Neo, and photography in general, is in exploring and developing your own style. There's no *right* way to create art. With the knowledge you've gained from this book, you're ready to explore, experiment, and create your unique vision.

Continue to explore, continue to create, and most importantly, continue to enjoy the process. Your artistry is a journey, not a destination, and Luminar Neo is a powerful companion to have at your side. Happy editing!

Nicole Young | nicolesy.com

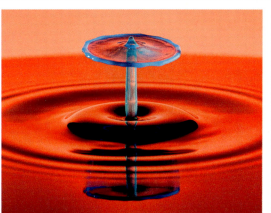

Conclusion 115

SHORTCUTS

This section includes a list of many common keyboard shortcuts found in Luminar Neo. For a full list of all shortcuts available, please visit the Skylum website: **manual.skylum.com**

GENERAL

DESCRIPTION	MAC	WINDOWS
Open file for quick edits	Cmd O	Ctrl O
Quit Luminar	Cmd Q	Ctrl W
Export image	Shift Cmd E	Shift Ctrl E
Page setup	Shift Cmd P	Shift Ctrl P
Print	Cmd P	Ctrl P
Zoom In	Cmd +	Ctrl +
Zoom Out	Cmd -	Ctrl -
Zoom to 100%	Cmd 1	Ctrl 1
Fit image to screen	Cmd 0	Ctrl 0
Toggle full-screen preview	F	N/A
Luminar Preferences	Cmd ,	Ctrl ,
Switch to Presets module	T	T
Reset adjustments	Shift Cmd R	Shift Ctrl R

CATALOG MODULE

DESCRIPTION	MAC	WINDOWS
Switch to Gallery view	**L**	**N/A**
Toggle Single image/Gallery views	**Space**	**Space**
Sync Adjustments	**Shift Cmd S**	**Shift Ctrl S**
Copy Adjustments	**Cmd C**	**Ctrl C**
Paste Adjustments	**Cmd V**	**Ctrl V**
Reset Adjustments	**Shift Cmd R**	**Shift Ctrl R**
Flag an image	**P**	**P**
Reject an image	**X**	**X**
Unmark an image	**U**	**U**
Search the Catalog	**Cmd F**	**Ctrl F**
Create a new Album	**Cmd N**	**Ctrl N**
Move image to Trash	**Cmd Delete**	**Ctrl Delete**
Remove from Album	**Delete**	**Delete**
Navigate to the next image	**Right Arrow**	**Right Arrow**
Navigate to the previous image	**Left Arrow**	**Left Arrow**

EDIT MODULE

DESCRIPTION	MAC	WINDOWS
Switch to Edit panel	E	E
Toggle before/after preview	\	\
Split-screen comparison preview	;	;
Toggle clipping	J	J
Crop	C	C
Change Crop orientation	X	X
Clone & Stamp	Cmd J	Ctrl J
Erase	Cmd E	Ctrl E
Rotate canvas left	Cmd [	Ctrl [
Rotate canvas right	Cmd]	Ctrl]

MASKING

DESCRIPTION	MAC	WINDOWS
Masking Brush	B	B
Linear Gradient mask	G	G
Radial Gradient mask	R	R
Increase Brush size	]	]
Decrease Brush size	[	[
Increase Brush softness	Shift]	Shift]
Decrease Brush softness	Shift [	Shift [
Invert mask	Cmd I	Ctrl I
Clear mask	Cmd Delete	N/A
Toggle paint modes (paint/erase)	X	X
Toggle red mask preview	/	N/A

INDEX

A

adjustment tools, 44–87
Adobe DNG converter, 51
Adobe Lightroom Classic, plugin, 107
Adobe Photoshop, plugin, 108
albums, 4, 15
Apple Photos, extension, 110
Atmosphere AI tool, 68

B

Background Removal AI extension, 96 | *See also Layer Properties*
batch processing, 112
Black & White tool, 56
blend modes, 35
blur background | *See Portrait Bokeh AI*
Body AI tool, 82
brush | *See masking, types*

C

Camera Profile | *See Develop tool*
    importing custom profiles, 51
catalog, 4, 6, 11, 14, 20, 28
    add photos to, 9–10
    auto backup, 7
    backing up, 8
    cache, 7
    create new, 6
    location, 7
    open catalog, 6
    open recent, 6
    restoring, 8
Catalog module, 4–19
    module overview, 4–5
chromatic aberration (removal), 100
chromatic aberrations (removal), 50
clear mask | *See mask actions*
clipping, 32
Clone tool, 87
cold pixels | *See clipping*
color balance | *See Color Harmony tool*
color contrast | *See Color Harmony tool*
Color Harmony tool, 85
color space | *See export*
Color tool, 55
Composition AI, 45
copy mask | *See mask actions*
Creative tools, 62–77
Crop AI, 45
CUBE file, 72
Curves, 47–48 | *See also Develop tool*
custom object composition, 104
cylindrical | *See projection modes*

D

dehaze | *See Landscape tool*
Denoise tool, 59
Details tool, 57–58

Develop tool, 46–51
    Blacks & Whites, 47
    Camera profile, 46
    Curves, 47–48
    Light adjustments, 47
    Noise Reduction, 50
    Optics, 50
    Sharpness adjustments, 49
    Transform adjustments, 51
    White Balance (color adjustments), 49
devignette, 99
Dodge & Burn tool, 86
Dramatic tool, 71

E

Edit module, 28–43
    workspace, 30
Edits panels, 30
Enhance AI tool, 52
Erase tool, 53
    objects removal, 53
Essentials Tools, 46–61
export, 4, 17, 20, 28, 113, 116
extensions, 2, 4, 20, 27, 28, 44, 88
Extensions installer, 4
eye enhancement, portrait | *See Face AI tool*
eye whitening | *See Face AI tool*

F

Face AI tool, 80
Face Enhancer | *See Upscale AI extension*
Face Enhancer AI | *See Supersharp AI extension*
Favorite tools, 81
fill mask | *See mask actions*
Film Grain tool, 77
fisheye | *See projection modes*
flag images, 17

flip image, 17, 45
Focus Stacking extension, 90–91
folders, 4, 14
foliage enhancer | *See Landscape tool*

G

gallery view, 18
ghost reduction, 89, 100
Glow tool, 76
grain, adding | *See Film Grain tool*
graphics processor, 7

H

HDR Merge extension, 88–89
HDR Panorama Stitching, 99
High Key tool, 83
histogram, 30–31
hot pixels | *See clipping*
HSL, 55 | *See also Color tool*

I

importing photos to the catalog | *See catalog, add photos to*
info panel, 4, 16
invert mask | *See mask actions*

L

Landscape tool, 60
Layer Properties, 35–36
    blend mode, 35
    opacity, 35
layers, 2–5, 28, 30, 33, 34, 39
    adding new, 33
    delete (remove), 34

duplicate, 34
hide layer, 34
layer actions, 34
mapping, 36
rearrange, 34
show layer, 34
transforming, 36
lens distortion (correction), 50, 99
Lightroom | *See Adobe Lightroom Classic, plugin*
linear gradient | *See masking, types*
LNPC file, 23, 26
LNP file, 25
location on computer, 7
lost edits, 13
Luminar menu, 4
LUTs | *See Mood tool*
LUTs, importing | *See Mood tool*

M

Magic Light AI extension, 95
mask actions, 43
   clear mask, 43
   copy mask, 43
   fill mask, 43
   invert mask, 43
   mask visibility, 43
   paste mask, 43
Mask AI, 42
masking, 37–43
   adjustment masking, 39
   layer masking, 38
   layer vs. adjustment, 38
   masking overview, 37
   tool masking, 39
masking, types, 40–43
   brush, 40
   linear gradient, 41

Mask AI, 42
   portrait background removal, 42
   radial gradient, 41
Matte tool, 74
menu, 4, 20
mercator | *See projection modes*
module selector, 4, 20, 28
Mood tool, 72
Mystical tool, 75

N

Noiseless AI extension, 93

O

opacity | *See Layer Properties*

P

panorama stitching, 98
   from video, 101–105
   photography tips, 98
paste mask | *See mask actions*
photo actions, 4, 19
Photos | *See Apple Photos, extension*
Photoshop | *See Adobe Photoshop, plugin*
plane | *See projection modes*
plugins, installing, 106
plugin, using Luminar Neo as, 106
portrait background removal, 42
Portrait Bokeh AI, 78
Portrait tools, 78–83
preferences, 7
preset amount slider, 24
presets
   applying, 24

categories, 22
creating, 27
for this photo, 22
importing, 25–26
my presets, 22
purchased, 23
workspace, 22
Presets module, 20–27
module overview, 20–21
Professional tools, 84–87
projection modes, 100

R

radial gradient | *See masking, types*
red eye removal | *See Face AI tool*
Relight AI tool, 62
remove color cast, 55 | *See also Color tool*
reset adjustments, 44
rotate image, 17, 45

S

saturation | *See Color tool*
search the catalog, 4, 11
settings | *See preferences*
share images, 17
shine removal | *See Skin AI tool*
Shortcuts (catalog), 4, 12
show mask | *See mask actions, mask visibility*
single image edits, 12, 111
single image view, 19
Skin AI tool, 81
Skin Defects Removal AI, 81
Sky AI tool, 63–67
Sky Enhancer AI, 52 | *See also Enhance AI tool*
sky reflection | *See Sky AI tool*
smart objects, 109

sort and filter, 4, 15
spherical | *See projection modes*
split color warmth | *See Color Harmony tool*
split toning | *See Toning tool*
Structure AI tool, 54
Sunrays tool, 69–70
Supercontrast tool, 84
Supersharp AI extension, 94
sync adjustments | *See batch processing*

T

teeth whitening | *See Face AI tool*
Toning tool, 73
tool masking | *See masking, adjustment masking*
Tools panels, 30
transpose image, 45
trash, 13

U

Upscale AI extension, 92

V

vibrance | *See Color tool*
video panorama stitching, 101–105
action panorama, 103–105
basic panorama, 102
custom object composition, 104
Vignette tool, 61

W

white balance, 49 | *See also Develop tool*

www.nicolesy.com

Made in the USA
Monee, IL
22 August 2023

41415396R00079